D0312520

PRAISE FOR
THE MAKING OF A MAN

Tim Brown was a great player, teammate, and friend. Now he's written *The Making of a Man*, which tells the story of his journey to the Heisman, the Raiders, and becoming an NFL star. More important, he tells what it means to become a man who makes a difference. This is a great read into the man behind the legend. I highly recommend this book.

— **MARCUS ALLEN**

Former Heisman Trophy Winner
NFL Hall of Fame Running Back and
Super Bowl XLVIII MVP

This honest and up close play-by-play of the amazing life of Tim Brown is a great read and a powerful, compelling testimony. The gift of this story will help men find the true north that God has for them.

— **C. JEFFREY WRIGHT**

CEO, UMI (Urban Ministries Inc.)

Over the years, I've respected Tim Brown as an NFL opponent, a teammate, and a friend. In *The Making of a Man*, you will read what has made Tim the man he is today and learn vital lessons on what being a man is all about. Whether young or old, every guy should read this book.

— **JERRY RICE**

NFL Hall of Fame Wide Receiver
Three-Time Super Bowl Champion

I've had the privilege of knowing Tim for over thirty years now. I've seen him beat the odds in many different areas of life, especially as a father and a mentor. I believe this book will help bring out your true greatness as you read stories about Tim's successes and struggles, and as you're inspired by his commitment to integrity as well as the life principles and the faith that have carried him through.

— **CAREY CASEY**

CEO, National Center for Fathering
fathers.com

THE
MAKING
OF A
MAN

THE
MAKING
OF A
MAN

How Men and Boys Honor God
and Live with Integrity

TIM BROWN

with

JAMES LUND

W PUBLISHING GROUP

AN IMPRINT OF THOMAS NELSON

Published in Nashville, Tennessee, by W Publishing, an imprint of Thomas Nelson.

Author is represented by the literary agency of Alive Communications, Inc., 7680 Goddard Street, Suite 200, Colorado Springs, CO 80920.

Thomas Nelson titles may be purchased in bulk for educational, business, fund-raising, or sales promotional use. For information, please e-mail SpecialMarkets@ThomasNelson.com.

Library of Congress Control Number: 2014903148

ISBN 978-0-8499-4757-5

Printed in the United States of America

14 15 16 17 18 RRD 6 5 4 3 2 1

This book is dedicated to Gene Brown, my father, the ultimate patriarch. We had our ups and downs, but God had a plan for both of us and it couldn't have turned out any better.

Pop, I would not have become the man I am today without your guidance. Even if I was scared of you half the time, whatever it took to get it done, you got it done. I am so grateful to be your son.

CONTENTS

Foreword   xi

Introduction   xiii

  1. A Man Is Thankful   1

  2. Mama Knows Best   11

  3. Manhood Starts with Dad   21

  4. A Man Uses His Skills   31

  5. Persistence Creates Confidence   43

  6. Men Need Mentors   57

  7. Even Heisman Winners Get Humbled   73

  8. A Man Takes Responsibility   83

  9. A Man Is Mentally and Physically Strong 93

10. A Man Overcomes Temptation   103

11. Faith Is for Life   113

CONTENTS

12. A Man Romances a Woman's Heart   123

13. Be Who You're Meant to Be   133

14. Surround Yourself with Good People   143

15. Respect Must Be Earned   153

16. Little Things Lead to Big Results   165

17. A Man Knows His Priorities   173

18. A Father Leads His Children   187

19. A Man Overcomes Evil   195

20. Your Legacy Matters   205

NFL Career Stats   213

Acknowledgments   215

Notes   219

About the Authors   221

FOREWORD

Years ago, when I took over as head football coach at the University of Notre Dame, it didn't take me long to see that Tim Brown had a special talent. I told him then I thought he could be the best player in the country. Once Tim caught that vision, he was on his way. Eighteen months after our first meeting, he and I were together at the New York Athletic Club, where he was presented the Heisman Trophy as the nation's top college player. Tim was the best and most intelligent player I ever coached.

Most people underestimate what they are capable of. This is why the task of raising expectations and inspiring people to reach for excellence falls to parents, teachers, and coaches. Some rebel against these efforts to bring out greatness. Others respond positively and thrive, achieving unprecedented levels of success. I was confident that Tim Brown would be the latter, and over the years he has proved me right time and again. His talent, confidence, competitiveness, and commitment allowed him to excel at the college level, made him a leader and a star with the NFL's Raiders, enabled him to set numerous league records, and propelled him to what was unquestionably a Hall of Fame career.

Tim was a great football player but what impresses me most is that he is an even better person. Like any man, he has confronted challenges and temptations and struggled at times in his life. Yet he emerged from that process a man of deep faith, high integrity, and strong values. He is dedicated to his God, his family, and his standards of what it means to live a winning life. I am honored to have coached him all those years ago and proud to call him a friend today. This is a man I respect, admire, and love.

We need men like Tim Brown in our world. Too many boys and teens lack a role model who can show them what being a man is all about. Too many fathers and leaders have forgotten or never learned what true manhood looks like. It isn't hard to find the bad examples—we see them in the news all the time. But if you look for them, the good ones are out there too. Tim is one of those guys. He is living a life of significance, helping others better themselves through word and deed.

Regardless of your age or gender, you will enjoy and benefit from reading this book. It is a fascinating look at the journey of one of football's all-time greats, yet it is also much more. If you or someone you love needs a blueprint for manhood, I can't think of a better place to start than *The Making of a Man*.

— Lou Holtz
Former Notre Dame Head
Coach and TV Analyst

INTRODUCTION

How do you make a man? You could say that I've been trying to answer that question all my life.

Every young boy dreams about growing up and becoming his vision of a man. To a boy, a man is probably a leader and a hero. He might be an astronaut, a cowboy, a soldier, a firefighter, or yes, a football player. He might also be a husband and father. When I was a boy, I imagined myself standing in a pulpit, delivering a stirring message as a preacher. That's not every young boy's idea of a man, but it was mine.

But what is manhood, really? How do us guys get there—and how do we know when we've arrived?

My answers started forming as I grew up in South and East Dallas with my parents, brother, and sisters. I added more pieces to the puzzle during all the stadium stops of my football career at

Notre Dame and with the Raiders in the National Football League. The picture grew clearer when I finally made a total commitment to God and my faith. Today, as a father, I'm guiding my sons as they ask the same question.

The need for an answer has never been greater—and not just for me and my family. Look around. We have ten million moms in America trying to raise their kids by themselves. We have teens who think being a man is getting a tattoo or driving a truck with oversized wheels. We have wives and girlfriends trying to figure out their men, and single gals without a clue of what they should be looking for in a man. And we've got millions of guys, young and old, single and husbands and dads, who after years of searching are *still* trying to understand what it takes to make a man.

I won't say that I've got it all figured out or that I haven't made mistakes along the way. Yet the blessings I've been given, especially my family, my football career, and my faith, have given me unique insights on the male perspective. What I have learned is that becoming a man is about a lot more than talking tough, trying to look cool, or scoring touchdowns. The answer has many layers, some fairly obvious and some much more subtle.

This book is my story. It takes you through the highs and lows of being a member of the Brown family and of being a Heisman Trophy winner and NFL All-Pro. But more than that, it's a look at the principles and priorities that have made me the man I am today—and that can make you, or someone you love, a man as well.

Let's get into it.

1

A MAN IS THANKFUL

There is always, always, always something to be thankful for.

ANONYMOUS

We lined up without a huddle. It was a hitch play, a zero-ninety audible. From the left side, I took a couple of steps then sprinted to my left. As usual, Rich Gannon's pass was on target. I caught it on our thirty-one yard line. A quick fake and I was past cornerback Samari Rolle. I got a block, then made another player miss.

Two guys came at me. Safety Tank Williams was on my left, defensive end Kevin Carter on my right. I'd already gained ten yards. I was usually good about getting down on the ground before a big hit, which is what I should have done this time. But there was a chance for just a little more, and in this game, I was ready to fight for every yard. I kept running.

Carter, all 290 pounds of him, got to me first. When he hit me, he punched the ball out of my right arm—a fumble. Rolle recovered. Just like that, we'd lost possession and maybe our momentum.

Correct that—*I'd* lost it. As I headed to the sideline, a television camera caught the pained look on my face. This was the biggest game of my life, and I was afraid I'd just blown it. It was January 19, 2003, and the Oakland Raiders were playing the Tennessee Titans for the American Football Conference championship. The winner would advance to the Super Bowl.

Twenty-five years is a long time to play the game of football. It feels even longer if during all those years you've never competed for a title, let alone walked off the field a champion. But that was exactly my situation. Starting with my days as a third grader at Dallas's Mount Auburn Elementary, and all the way through middle school, high school, college, and fifteen years as a pro, I'd been on a lot of losing teams. I had never had the opportunity to even try to win it all. I wanted it bad. Now, in a crazy place known for the notorious "Black Hole" and its rowdy fans, I hoped to finally get my chance.

I woke up that morning at the Oakland Airport Hilton thinking about everything that had brought me to this point. It had been a great season for the Raiders. We'd started fast, winning our first four games, then dropped the next four, two of them in overtime. But we turned it on in the season's second half, winning seven of our last eight, followed by a 30–10 victory over the New York Jets in the playoffs.

We had an incredible offense, led by Rich Gannon, the league's Most Valuable Player that year and the most mentally prepared quarterback I ever played with, as well as my good friend Jerry Rice, the NFL's all-time leader in receptions and yardage, and All-Pro linemen Lincoln Kennedy and Barret Robbins. On defense, our leaders were guys like All-Pro safety Rod Woodson and longtime standouts Charles Woodson and Bill Romanowski. Now we were one step away from playing on Super Sunday.

I'd come close to the big game before.

Actually, after my rookie year, I ended up watching the San Francisco 49ers win the Super Bowl from the same suite as Raiders owner Al Davis. That's where I decided I wouldn't be attending the Super Bowl in person again until I got there as a player. It was too tough seeing those guys celebrate on the field. That was where *I* wanted to be.

My first real chance at the big one came in 1990, my third year in the NFL. The Raiders won their division and advanced to the AFC title game. Then the Buffalo Bills destroyed us, 51–3. A decade later, in 2000, we were division champs again. This time it was the Baltimore Ravens and their swarming defense that stopped us in the AFC championship, 16–3.

And then came 2001 and the infamous "Tuck Rule Game." Once again, we were in the AFC title game, this time against the New England Patriots. We were protecting a three-point lead late in the game when we recovered a Patriots fumble, apparently sealing a trip to the Super Bowl at last. But the officials reversed their call, citing an obscure rule. New England kicked a field goal to tie the game, then another in overtime to win it. We felt robbed, that the league had it in for us. You can't imagine the anger and disappointment after that one.

But now, a season later, we were back. At this point I was thirty-six years old, practically ancient in the world of football. In just my second year in the NFL, I suffered a knee injury that caused me to miss virtually the whole season. Doctors told me then I'd be fortunate to play until I was thirty. Despite this, I'd survived fifteen years in the league. I guess some would say "thrived." I'd been named to nine Pro Bowls. I'd led the league in receptions one year, in kick return yards and average in another, and in punt return yards in a third. I had the second-most receiving yards in NFL history.

It had been a great run, but you could say that I was playing on borrowed time. It was another reason why I wanted so badly to get to the Super Bowl.

Yet I'd also changed during those fifteen years. My life was about more than me and football. My faith had matured and deepened. I'd always believed in God, but now I was fully committed to Him. As a husband and father, I became more devoted to my family than ever. I was becoming the man I was meant to be.

One look at Sherice, my beautiful wife, was all it took to remind me of the joys and responsibilities that extended far beyond the NFL. We had been married for nearly six years, and already had a daughter together. Now she was eight and a half months pregnant, expecting twins. If that doesn't make you think about who you are and where you're headed, I don't know what will. So much of my past had centered around myself and football, but my future was all about my wife, my kids, and our expanding family.

I didn't want it any other way.

Not that I'd lost my competitive fire. No chance. Individual awards are great, but especially at this point in my football career, my focus was on wins. The Super Bowl was the only thing missing from my resumé, and everyone around me knew it.

When Jerry Rice left the San Francisco 49ers and joined the Raiders the season before, he said, "I came over here for one reason—that's to help Tim Brown win the Super Bowl." I was definitely on board with that. I wanted all the help I could get.

As far as help from above, I was open to that too, but I no longer prayed to win specific games. That never felt right to me. If I'm praying to win and the other team is doing the same thing, then what? But I did pray for strength, for my teammates and I to play our best, and for good health when the game was over. And early in my career, I also prayed, "Lord, help me win a Super Bowl. Show me how I can help win a Super Bowl."

In the last few years, though, my perspective and prayer had changed. I was trying to leave the winning and losing up to God. I just wanted to be there, to go through that whole experience. If I could just play in the big game, it would be something no one could ever take away from me.

———————

Spaghetti with meat sauce. Toast with butter and honey. That's what was on my plate at the hotel before the Tennessee game, because that's what I always ate before a late-day game. Athletes depend on routine to help them stay focused, and I was no exception. If the honey for my toast was missing, there was going to be trouble!

During my rookie year, whenever we played in one of the late games scheduled on a Sunday, I always watched the first five or ten minutes of the early TV game in my hotel room. When my second season began, however, I'd been named a starter, and I was so excited about being on the field for that opening game that I broke my routine. I left the hotel earlier than usual, missing the start of the early game on TV.

That was the day I injured my knee. After one catch, I was out for the year.

I was sure I got hurt because I'd changed my usual pregame schedule. So for the rest of my career, whenever we played in the late game, I always watched the kickoff and at least the first series of the early game. Now that we were facing the Titans in the AFC title game, I sure wasn't going to mess with my routine.

Of course, on this day my interest in the early game was more than casual. We might be playing the winner in the Super Bowl. So after my spaghetti, I watched the favored Philadelphia Eagles score an early touchdown, then saw the Tampa Bay Buccaneers come back with a field goal, a seventy-one-yard completion to Joe Jurevicius, and a touchdown by Mike Alstott to take a 10–7 lead.

Time to go. I had my own game to play.

The drive to Oakland's Network Associates Coliseum took only six or seven minutes. Tens of thousands of fans were already there and waiting to get in, many lined up along the lane into the players' parking lot. They were pumped up, shouting and waving. I knew that when all sixty thousand–plus fans arrived the atmosphere in the stadium was going to be even crazier.

It was loud in the locker room too, but as usual I was ignoring all that. I got into my undergarments, put headphones over my ears and a towel over my head, and turned on my gospel music, people like Fred Hammond, Donnie McClurkin, and Yolanda Adams. It was my way to tune out the world and begin focusing on what I needed to do.

On this day, I was having a little trouble with that focus. The demons that had haunted all those past Raiders teams were threatening to get into my head. I needed to forget all that negativity and not think about what could go wrong, how one bad call or one bad play could turn everything against us. It was time to be positive. After all, we were a confident, veteran team. We'd led the NFL in total yards. We were favored and had the home field. If we avoided mental mistakes, we would get it done.

I turned up my music and walked to the training room to get taped up: ankles, wrists, and my big toes to prevent turf toe. Then it was back to my locker, where I lay on my back on the carpeted floor, stretched my hands out, and thought through our plays, my routes for each play, and the film we'd watched of Tennessee. For the next twenty-five minutes, I let my body relax while I prepared my mind for what was coming.

I stretched for another half hour, then applied heated plaster patches to my back, hamstrings, and hip flexors—the temperature at kickoff would be forty-eight degrees, and I knew it would be a lot colder by game's end. Once I got my pads and pants on, it was 2:00 p.m., ninety minutes before kickoff. It was time to warm up on the field.

The fans were streaming in, including in sections 104, 105, 106, and 107 in the south end zone, otherwise known as the Black Hole. This is where the most rabid followers resided, all standing up, all decked out in silver and black and crazy costumes: pirates, gorillas, Darth Vader, you name it. Raider Nation has always been made up of the wildest, most enthusiastic, most supportive fans anywhere. I hoped this would be the day we rewarded them.

We came out firing. After the kickoff, Rich Gannon connected with Jerry Rice on a twenty-nine-yard pass. I caught the next one for twelve yards. Then it was a pass to Charlie Garner for six yards and another to me for fourteen, which put us on Tennessee's eight yard line. After a pair of runs, Gannon hit Jerry Porter with a three-yard touchdown pass.

Just like that, we were up 7–0. It looked like the Titans couldn't stop us.

I knew it wasn't going to be that easy, though, and it wasn't. They came right back, with Steve McNair passing thirty-three yards to Drew Bennett for the game-tying touchdown. We marched down the field a second time and scored again on a twelve-yard completion to Garner. Gannon had yet to throw an incomplete pass.

Early in the second quarter, our defense held the Titans to a field goal. We were up 14–10 to start our next drive. Our offense was clicking. It was just like I'd figured in the locker room—all we had to do was avoid mistakes and not beat ourselves.

And that's when I fumbled.

I won't say I was thinking, *Here we go again,* as I walked off the field. But I definitely hoped our defense would stop Tennessee on that next drive. The last thing I wanted was to make it easy for the Titans to get the edge on us. Fumbles can turn a game around.

Our guys did hold them—Roderick Coleman dropped running back Eddie George for a six-yard loss on second down—and I shook plenty of hands as our defense left the field. Only we didn't do anything with the ball either, and on their next possession, the Titans drove it in, scoring a touchdown on McNair's nine-yard scramble.

We'd crushed Tennessee earlier in the season, 52–25. But now, in the biggest game of the season and of my career, with 2:54 to go in the half, the Titans led 17–14. We had to respond.

Our situation looked even worse when, after a short pass and two incompletions, we had to punt. But like I said, fumbles can turn a game around. As it turned out, it wasn't my fumble that made the difference, but a pair by Tennessee.

The first came with 1:38 to play. Running back Rob Holcombe tried a spin move up the middle, but Eric Barton hit him and knocked the ball loose. Anthony Dorsett recovered on the Tennessee sixteen, and two plays later we had a touchdown to take back the lead, 21–17.

Then our kickoff coverage team turned in a huge play. Peter Simon made a strong kick return for the Titans, but he coughed up the ball on a tackle by Tim Johnson. There was a scramble for the ball before Alvis Whitted fell on it. We had the ball on Tennessee's thirty-nine yard line. Gannon scrambled for fourteen yards on first down, and we ended up with a field goal on the last play of the half to lead 24–17.

The game was still tight after three quarters, as we led 27–24. But we finally played the way we were capable of, scoring on a sixty-six-yard drive, forcing a Tennessee punt, and driving another sixty-nine yards. When running back Zack Crockett rushed that last seven yards into the end zone, there was only 3:29 left in the game. We were up 41–24. The crowd roared louder than I'd ever heard them.

I'd led both teams with nine receptions on the day, for seventy-three yards, but I didn't care about that. As I walked off the field, emotions overwhelmed me. *This is really happening. We're going to the Super Bowl.*

The guys on the sideline were whooping it up, but I was barely holding it together. Freddie Biletnikoff, the great Raiders receiver who was now our receivers coach, gave me a hug. That put it over the top. The tears started flowing. All I could do was grab a towel and put it over my head again. After all these years, after all the training and practices and injuries and heartbreaking losses, I'd finally made it to the big game. I was just so thankful.

I thought about Sherice and the kids and how much I loved them. I thought about Mama and Dad, my brother and sisters, and all the support my family had given me. I remembered my pastor and others at our church, my friends, my teammates, Raiders fans, everyone who had played a part in my journey to this point.

As the seconds on the scoreboard clock ticked away, more players and staff from the Raiders kept coming up to congratulate me. Jerry Rice gave me a hug and said, "I told you we were going to get there!"

Was I excited and thrilled? Of course. But even more than that, I was thankful. *Thank You, God,* I silently prayed. *Thank You for all the people You've put in my life. Thank You for this win, this team, and this opportunity. Thank You.*

In the good times of my life—and there have been many—I've always tried to remember to thank God for what He's given me. I've met many people who are extremely successful in their careers. Some of them, once they start talking, are pretty quick to tell you about all they've done. It's "I, I, I" and "Me, me, me." They have a difficult time acknowledging the people who helped them along the way. More important, they fail to give God the credit for opening the doors to opportunity and giving them the skills to succeed. They want to believe their accomplishments are all the result of their hard work. And sure, they've put in the work. But none of it would matter if God wasn't paving the road ahead.

That's not the attitude I want to have, which is why I was quick to thank God after our victory over Tennessee. He'd always been faithful to me, and on one of the great days of my life, I wanted to be sure I remained faithful to Him. That, I believe, is what a man does.

Naturally, it's much easier to be thankful when times are good, whether it's after a big raise at work or after you win a game that puts you in the Super Bowl. The challenge is to be just as thankful when your job gets eliminated or you get cut from the team. The blessings are harder to see at those times. It can seem as if God is on vacation just when you need Him most.

God has a perspective we don't, however. He has a purpose for what He does. He often allows us to go through a bad season on the gridiron or in life in order to get us to the place where He really wants us to be. Even when we can't see it, He's got it under control.

The Bible says, "Give thanks in all circumstances; for this is God's will for you in Christ Jesus" (1 Thess. 5:18). That's a great verse for any man. To me, it's one of the first and most important steps toward manhood—remembering to always be grateful to God and the people who care about you.

2

MAMA KNOWS BEST

Men are what their mothers made them.

RALPH WALDO EMERSON

When I look back on my life, I feel blessed in so many ways. One of those blessings is that I survived my childhood.

My mother brought me into the world on July 22, 1966, at Parkland Memorial Hospital, the same Dallas hospital where President Kennedy had been declared dead three years earlier. My parents named me Timothy Donell—Timothy after the Bible figure and Donell because my mother liked the name. The delivery was smooth enough, but it wasn't long before I gave the rest of my family plenty to worry about.

I was six months old and crawling around the house when I pulled on an electrical cord that hung from our ironing board. My sister had left the iron out, and it was still hot. That iron fell on the right side of my head and then scalded my left arm.

The Brown family didn't have much in the way of funds, so

nobody took me to the doctor—at first. Then, when the burn on my arm became infected and my whole body swelled up like a balloon, I was rushed to the hospital. I was having trouble getting air. For a time, it didn't look good. The doctors were a few hours away from surgically inserting a tube into my neck so I could breathe.

Anyone who knows Josephine Brown understands that she wouldn't take news like that without doing something about it. My mom got her dad and brother down to the hospital, and they immediately set up a prayer vigil in the waiting room near my room. I don't know what they said to God. All I know is that three or four hours later, the nurse came up to them and said, "We think Tim's doing better." I recovered just fine, though today I have an iron-shaped scar on my arm and don't hear as well out of my right ear.

According to my mom, that day of the prayer vigil and my quick turnaround in the hospital was when she first knew I was going to be "special."

I'm not so sure about special, but I do believe God must have a purpose for my life, because that wasn't the last close call He got me through. When I was four, I found a matchbook. Naturally, I decided it would be a good idea to get some newspaper and start a fire. I lit it on our back porch, and soon the screen to our back door was in flames. Fortunately, a neighbor ran into the house and fetched my mom, who put it out. My dad whipped me pretty good for that one.

Then there was the day about a year later that I found a bullet in the yard across the street. I just happened to have a hammer in my hand. Why was I walking around the neighborhood with a hammer? Don't ask me. But since I had it, I decided to use it. I slammed it down on the bullet, once . . . twice—

Crack!

The bullet exploded, hitting me in the forehead. I fell down.

The neighbors came rushing out of their house, sure I'd just killed myself. But the only lasting effect was a scar on my head.

It's near the one I later got from a scrape with a dog.

I seemed pretty determined to do bodily harm to myself in those days. But I wasn't the only one. When she was seven and I was five, my sister Gwen got angry with me and decided to end my earthly existence. It may have had something to do with me smacking her.

Gwen's plan was pretty elaborate for a seven-year-old. She wedged a knife into the ground in our front yard, the point sticking straight up. Then she got a brick and placed it in a strategic spot in front of the knife. She proceeded to chase me through the yard, right toward her trap. And her plan nearly worked. I did trip on the brick and fall on the knife. But the point stuck into my knee—painful, but not fatal. (In case you're wondering, Gwen and I are much better friends today—it's been years since she's tried to kill me.)

Maybe all those early narrow escapes were the inspiration for my ability to dodge would-be tacklers on the football field. Too often, it seemed, I was eluding trouble just in time.

The neighborhood we lived in probably didn't help. For the first seven years of my life, my family's home was 4315 Copeland Street, a small, two-bedroom apartment in a rundown fourplex in South Dallas. "The Hood" was the kind of area where my dad made sure to let people know he had guns in the house, just in case anyone got ideas about robbing or hassling us.

My parents didn't buy their children a lot of toys or the fancy gadgets so many kids take for granted these days. I didn't have my own bedroom, so I either shared a bed or slept on the floor. But we always had what we needed. I never thought we were lower class or that we lived in a bad neighborhood. It was just life, and actually, it was pretty good.

The biggest reason I felt that way was my family. My dad was away most of the time, working as a construction foreman during the day and managing a nightclub in the evening. But I had my two uncles and their families living right next to us in the same fourplex. I had my sisters Joyce (nearly eleven years older), Ann (four years older), and Gwen. I had my brother, Wayne (eight years older).

And most of all, I had Mama.

———

Josephine Kelly grew up in Louisiana, the daughter of a Baptist preacher. She was the youngest of seven kids. Early on, she absorbed the idea from both her parents that family was terribly important.

My mother was twelve when she met my dad, who was seventeen. He didn't have a car back then—he visited her by riding a horse named Chester. Mama was just eighteen when she married Eugene Brown, my dad. They already had two kids together. They were awfully young to be raising a family, and both had strong opinions about how to do it. Mama says they used to go at it, shouting at each other when they disagreed about something. She even waved a pot and pan at him a time or two, though she never actually hit him.

But just a year or so after they got married, my mom gave her heart to the Lord, and everything changed. She decided that from that point on, she would live right by God. That's exactly what she did. The crazy fights stopped. In fact, in all my life I never saw her argue with my dad. Just as important, she set out to give her children the best foundation she possibly could. All of us Brown kids knew that my dad was the voice of authority when he was around, but Mama was the one who held our family together and made sure things ran smoothly.

My earliest memories of my mother are of watching her get off the bus at the stop down the street. I was only three or four years old. She used to work as a seamstress for another family, and Gwen and I watched from our street corner when Mama was due to return home in the afternoon. I'd get so excited when I spotted that familiar hairdo with the part in the middle and little curl in the back. We'd both run to greet her, then walk with her back home.

Whether she was riding the bus or working at home, you never saw Mama in anything but a dress. It was always modest, not too tight and not too short. To this day, in fact, I've never seen her knees!

That was how she lived—modest. You never heard her boasting about anything, and she made sure her kids didn't brag either. She wasn't one for big speeches. She just quietly went about her day, cleaning and cooking for our family or sewing for another family to bring in some income.

Not that she was a pushover. No way. My dad was usually the disciplinarian when we kids got out of line, even if we had to wait for him to get home to find out what would happen to us. But Mama knew how to make her point when she needed to.

I still remember one time when I went too far with her. It was a hot summer day, and she stood at the sink in our tiny kitchen, preparing a meal. "Mama," I whined repeatedly, "can you give me thirty cents to go swimming?"

"Boy, you know I don't have thirty cents," she said. "You just go on out of here."

"Mama, c'mon," I said. "Give me thirty cents."

I don't know how she did it—I don't think she even looked at me—but her backhand was like a striking cobra. Before I knew it, the side of my face was stinging.

"Ow, Mama!" I said. "You didn't have to do that!"

"I told you to get out of here," she said, "and you're going to mess with me?"

That was the end of that conversation. You didn't mess with Mama. Not then, and not today.

I have so much respect for my mother. She did not have an easy life. Her marriage was not easy. Raising six children—the youngest, Kathy, was born sixteen years after me—was not easy. Working to provide enough dollars to pay for food and clothes while also running a household was not easy. Yet she never complained. She, along with my dad, did what was necessary to give her children the foundation they needed for a successful life.

Most important of all, she made sure we spent time with God.

———

For the Brown family, church was not something we did now and then when we felt the need for a little spiritual encouragement. It was a way of life. Mama insisted on it, and though Dad only showed up on Easter, he completely supported her program for the family. If there was any hesitation on my part, he was quick to tell me, "You are going to church, boy."

Actually, I didn't need much prodding. Unlike a lot of younger kids, I looked forward to church. I probably spent more time there than I did in my own home. During my first years, we attended Victory Chapel, a tiny church pastored by my uncle, Johnnie Grant. It served three extended families, and with only three rows of pews, sat thirty-five people tops.

What we lacked in numbers, we made up for in hours. We were there Wednesday nights, Friday nights, and all of Sunday—and I do mean *all*. I also remember youth "shut-in" services that started at 7:00 p.m. Friday and ran until 7:00 a.m. Saturday. Other times of the year, the church hosted revival services that ran all week.

Through rain, ice, snow, and sunshine, the Browns (minus Dad) were there for all of it. My mom got us involved in the church choir. When I was six, I also started playing the drum for the choir. Not "drums," as in a drum set, but "the drum." The rhythm section for our church's musical efforts was a single snare drum. The first time I saw someone playing a full drum set, I was blown away. *That guy can play five or six drums at once,* I thought. *He must be really talented.*

More important than all that was the Bible teaching we received at church. Before I was eight years old, I'd memorized all the books of the Bible, the Beatitudes, the Lord's Prayer, and Psalm 23. I didn't understand all of it, but I spent so much time on it that I couldn't help absorbing a portion of spiritual wisdom. It probably helped that I was competitive. Our Sunday school teacher was my grand-father, Mama's dad. He had us compete against each other to see who'd memorized their lesson the best. The winner got a six-pack of soda pop. Even then, I loved to win and taste that soda pop.

When I was twelve, we started attending Victory Temple Church of God in Christ in the Pleasant Grove area. That was a big change, since attendance probably averaged 350 people those first years. What didn't change, though, was that we practically lived at church.

As kids, we did take breaks now and then. After services let out on Sunday afternoons, my friends and I walked either to the Shake, Rattle, and Roll to ride go-karts or to the nearby middle school, where we practiced our dunks on eight-foot rims. Then, tired and sweaty, it was back to church for a snack and evening services.

Did I ever think about skipping out on church so I could mess around on my own? No. I *wanted* to be there. That's where my fam-ily was, literally and spiritually. These were the people who loved me and were looking out for me. And though I didn't comprehend it all, I knew what I was learning there about God was important.

Most of all, especially during those early years, I knew us being in church was top priority for Mama. The last thing I wanted was to disappoint her.

Mama didn't just get us to church and then sit back. She was active as a church missionary, which in our congregation meant that she might talk with people in the community as a representative of the church or visit people in need. Her commitment to living a godly life is another example of what made her, and still makes her, so amazing.

———

Every mother is special. I have great admiration for all moms. Each is a full-time doctor, psychologist, pastor, teacher, chef, taxi driver, and police officer, all rolled into one. Mothers love their children with a fierce devotion that no one else on the planet can match. And even though we sometimes pretend otherwise, we—their sons—need them.

Years ago, a Harvard University study found that 91 percent of men who didn't have a close relationship in their early years with their mothers eventually developed coronary artery disease, hypertension, ulcers, and alcoholism. Only 45 percent of men who were close to their moms had similar illnesses.[1] That tells me that mothers have a huge and lasting influence on the lives of their sons—not just on their health, but on every aspect of life.

I know that was the case for me. Mama was always there, steady as a compass pointing north. It's not that we did a lot together—she hardly had time with everything else that had to be done. And she didn't fill my head each day with wise sayings to guide me, which was probably a good thing. I know of parents who try too hard, always telling their kids what to do or attempting to teach them a lesson every minute. That can be too much, so that a son or daughter tunes the parent out as soon as mom or dad starts speaking.

Mama was more subtle than that. Once, for example, I was having trouble with a girlfriend. Mama could see that this girl had me twisted around, that I'd started to let her up-and-down emotions run my life. I couldn't see it, but Mama knew.

Instead of lecturing me or telling me this girl was a bad influence, she just said, "Timmy, didn't you tell me you met a nice young lady at your job?"

"Yes," I said.

"Well, why don't you go out to dinner with her?"

I thought for a second. "You know what?" I said. "That's a good idea, Mama."

My mother wasn't trying to break me and my girlfriend up. She just wanted to change the way I viewed that relationship, to put us back on equal terms. That was Mama—a world of good advice wrapped in a few simple words.

It wasn't Mama's words, however, that spoke most to me while I was growing up. It was the way she lived her life. Even then I understood that she was a woman of integrity. I never saw her say one thing and then do another. What you saw was who she was—a woman devoted to her God, her church, and her family. For her, as long as she could keep going to church and keep praying and fasting, everything was going to be all right.

That was an example I desperately needed, especially in later years when the temptations of the NFL lifestyle began coming my way. Mama set the bar high for herself and her family, yet I never saw her stumble. Sometimes my siblings and I kid her: "C'mon, Mama, can't you slip up once in a while?" But she hasn't while I've been watching. If she can live with that kind of faith and integrity, I guess I should be able to find a way to do that too.

No mother is perfect, of course. They all make mistakes, saying or doing or not doing things they later regret. A few fail consistently. Yet I believe all mothers love their children. And in the case of their sons, I believe each leaves an individual legacy that can help guide them. For me, it was Mama's commitment to faith and family, her steady presence, her wise counsel at just the right moments, and her example. For you, it might be something else. If you look for it, it's there for you to discover, grow from, and grab hold of for the rest of your life.

3

MANHOOD STARTS
WITH DAD

He didn't tell me how to live; he lived, and let me watch him do it.

CLARENCE BUDINGTON KELLAND

Y ou've probably figured out by now how much I love and admire my mom. I felt the same about my dad, but our relationship was a little more complicated.

My father, Eugene Brown, grew up in Monroe, Louisiana, the oldest of ten kids. By the time he met my mom, he was in many ways the man of the house. His mother had a stroke and was confined to a wheelchair, so he had to quit high school during his freshman year to help support the family. In those days, that meant working long hours in the fields picking cotton. His father worked in the fields too, so he pretty much put my dad in charge of raising his brothers and sisters. Then my dad started having kids, got married, and had his own family to handle too.

It was a lot of responsibility for a young man. I think my dad saw it as just doing what had to be done. It's where he first developed his amazing work ethic, and his lifelong ability to manipulate and fix things with his hands. He used to tell me he didn't want me laboring with my hands as he had. I kidded him about that after I got to the NFL: "Pop, I'm working with my hands, just not the way you did."

After his third child was born, my dad moved the family to Dallas in 1962, hoping for better opportunities. By the time I came along, his routine was set. Every weekday morning, he was out of the house by six thirty and on his way to his job as a construction crew foreman. Then, sometime between four fifteen and four forty-five every afternoon, his blue Buick Riviera rolled down the street and into our driveway. He'd plop into his easy chair for a few minutes, take a shower, watch *NBC Nightly News*, eat dinner, and take a nap. Then he was off to his second job, managing the Chandlelite nightclub he owned on Dolphin Street. I was nearly always in bed by the time he got home.

The weekends were just as consistent. Even after we moved away from the little fourplex on Copeland, Saturday was Dad's day to hang out with his "boys" from the old neighborhood. He and his buddies would sit under a tree, drink beer, and tell story after story. Sunday was his day at home. While the rest of us spent the day at church, he puttered around the house. During football season, he always watched his favorite NFL team on TV—the Cowboys, of course. Even after I joined the Raiders, his team was still the Cowboys. Like his routine, some things with my dad never changed.

———

My dad was what I call "a man's man." He wasn't a big guy, probably five foot ten, but when he walked into a room, people stopped what they were doing to hear what Gene Brown had to say. He carried himself with an air of authority. For us kids—or for anyone else—there was no whining or negotiating once he'd spoken. If Dad announced that we were going to spend the evening standing on our heads, then that's what we did.

Like my mother, Dad wasn't one for a lot of talk. He was all about instruction, not conversation. I'm sure that came from so often taking charge of a household with nine siblings. He saw it as his duty to make sure everyone was doing what they needed to do.

I remember one evening when I walked into a room and saw my dad repeatedly slapping one of his brothers, who was sitting at a table, on the back of his head. Dad said, "Don't you treat your wife like that. Don't you put your hands on her." His brother didn't argue or try to fight back. He just covered his head and said, "Okay, Gene. All right, Gene." As far as I know, that put an end to that issue.

That's how it was with my dad. If he saw or heard about a problem, he took care of it. And everyone respected him for it.

Dad wouldn't hesitate to put his kids in their place either. Growing up, I didn't get in trouble with him very often, but when I did it didn't take long for that belt to come out. Even worse, he was ambidextrous. When one hand got tired, he'd just switch to the other.

I'll never forget the last whipping of my life. It happened when I was eleven. In fact, it was the same summer day that Mama backhanded me for whining to her about the swimming money. By then, we'd moved to our two-bedroom house on Culver Street, on a hill in East Dallas. After getting nowhere with my mother, I'd gone outside and sat on the crumbling cement steps that led to our front door. Feeling frustrated, I began pitching rocks across the street.

I noticed a dog with only three legs walking down the street in my direction. *You know*, I thought, *it would be interesting to see what a three-legged dog looks like when he runs.*

I took aim and fired a rock toward the dog. I wasn't trying to hurt him, just scare him enough to get him moving, but that rock hit him square on the leg. The next moment, that poor dog wasn't walking or running, but crawling.

Unfortunately, old Mr. Mack, a Baptist preacher, was sitting on his porch watching the whole thing. He got up and walked over to me, shaking his head. "Tim," he said, "I'm not even going to deal with you about this. I'm going to tell your momma and tell your daddy."

Oh, no, please, I thought. *I'm already in trouble today.*

But that's just what happened. They both heard about it. After my dad got home, the two of them went at me, Dad with the belt and Mama with her words. "Timmy, all you have to do"—*slap!*—"is do what we ask you to do"—*slap!*—"and you'll never get in trouble."

Later, after I'd finished crying and thought for a bit, I went back to Mama. "Were you serious about what you said?" I asked. "To stay out of trouble, all I have to do is what you ask?"

"That's all, Timmy."

The light bulb went on in my head. *I can do that.*

That was the end of my encounters with Dad's belt, but it wasn't the last time he and I would square off.

———

Dad loved to sing in the car and around the house. He had a booming baritone voice. It was always the blues, something from Johnny Taylor or maybe B. B. King. In keeping with the blues lifestyle, he also smoked, drank, and cursed.

Seeing how Dad lived his life, and that he didn't go to church with us, really upset me. I realized that he didn't know God and that he wasn't moving any closer to Him.

One time during an all-night prayer session at church, we all got on our knees to talk to God. Pretty soon I noticed that a bunch of the other kids, including my sister, were crying. I figured I needed to cry too, so I thought about my dad, and soon the tears flowed. The thought of my father not going to heaven was the saddest thing in my life.

Maybe I also should have been sad about the fact that he and I rarely spent time together. We never played catch in the yard or went to a ballgame. But that was just how it was. He was working to take care of all of us, and that was top priority.

I remember only a couple of times when just the two of us did something together while I was growing up. One was when he took me fishing. The other was a crazy scheme when I was ten.

Someone had talked my dad into the idea that I could be a child fashion model. Who knows why he fell for that one, but he did. Mama wanted nothing to do with it. She said, "Gene, you know better. Why are you doing this? Why're you wasting your money?"

"No, Josephine," he said, "you'll see. He's going to make it."

So that Saturday, Mama got me dressed in my only good outfit—a green leisure suit—and Dad and I climbed into the Riviera for a day in downtown Dallas. We visited one photo studio after another, each seedier than the last. I'd pose on a bench or a chair while the photographer snapped photos and my dad looked on, apparently seeing dollar signs in his eyes.

The only people who ever made money from that outing were the photographers, but I never complained about it. They supplied me with M&M's and Snickers bars while I "modeled," and I got to spend a whole day with my dad—it was great! It also provided our family with a good story. Whenever we needed to lighten the mood, one of my brothers or sisters would say, "Hey, you remember the day when Daddy took Timmy on that modeling thing?"

Mama would chime in, "Gene, what were you thinking anyway?" My dad just chuckled. The fact that he didn't defend himself made it even funnier, because he usually had an opinion on everything.

What happened a couple of years later between my dad and me, however, wasn't funny at all. It was late June, when I was almost thirteen. It was a typical night at our home—Mama and my sisters were asleep, my older brother was in his room in the converted garage, and I was lying on the couch in the den, up late watching television. With the entrance to the den behind me, it would have been easy for anyone walking in to think I was asleep.

I didn't hear my dad come home, but suddenly there he was, back from Chandlelite. He turned off the TV, killing all the light in the room.

"Hey Pop, I'm still watching it!" I bellowed. I got up to turn the TV back on.

Maybe it was the shock of that shout out of the darkness. Maybe he thought I wanted to fight. Maybe he'd just had too much to drink. Whatever it was, I'd pushed him over the edge.

"You coming after me?" he screamed. "I am gonna kill you!"

The shouts continued as he charged back outside and opened the trunk of the car. "I'm getting my gun and I'm going to kill you!"

I knew he had guns in the trunk because I'd seen them many times. My sisters and I used to scope out his trunk for loose change. While my father took a nap, Ann stood guard at his bedroom and Gwen kept watch from the kitchen window. I'd jump in the trunk and grab a few coins out of a bucket, my heart racing. I was always careful not to touch the two pistols, one lying on each side of the bucket.

Now, with my dad's rage spilling over like lava from a volcano, my heart beat even faster. "Mama, come help!" I yelled. I scrambled into the corner of the den between the TV and the couch, scared for my life. My dad routinely came home with alcohol in his blood and on his breath, but I'd never seen it make him violent. I'd never seen him lay a hand on my mother. Did he really plan to kill me?

At that moment, it seemed entirely possible.

The shouts woke everyone. Mama came rushing out to the driveway. Fortunately, either because it was too dark, he was too drunk, or Mama's quiet words began to sink in, my dad didn't find the gun. He started to calm down, at least enough to stop shouting threats that the whole neighborhood could hear.

He didn't say another word to me that night. I continued to cower in the corner, afraid, confused, and increasingly angry. What had I done to deserve this? Was he crazy? I vowed right then to never take a sip of alcohol if it made you want to kill your own son.

In many ways, both positive and negative, that incident changed my life. For years, none of us in the family said a word about it. We all pretended that it hadn't happened. But inside, I was torn up.

My dad and I had a pretty good relationship up to that night. But now I was mad at him, and he was different with me too. He told me at least a couple of times over the next two years, "You're never going to amount to anything."

I thought about taking revenge—tampering with his tea or leaving nails behind the tires of the Riviera. I could have let my anger out through physical violence or tried to dull the fear and rejection I felt through drugs or my own drinking. Thankfully, I didn't choose any of those options.

I actually used my anger as fuel for succeeding in the classroom, and later in sports. I wanted my dad to see that he was wrong about me and about how he'd treated me that night. I wanted to hear, "I'm sorry." My grades were high, but I never did get that apology.

The anger and hurt from that period was something that stayed with me for a long time. It would be many years before it was truly resolved. Even so, I still loved my dad and was still proud to call him my father. He was a good man who had a bad night.

———————

Every boy dreams of growing up to be a man, in every sense of the word. Figuring out what that looks and sounds like might be the primary mission of boyhood. The first place he's going to look is his dad.

As I write this, my son Timothy Jr. is ten years old. He looks a lot like I did at his age, and probably acts a lot like me too, ready to pick up a ball and play a game on a moment's notice.

Timothy is like me in another way—he's always watching and listening to his dad. He probably doesn't realize it yet, but he's trying to figure out what it means to be a man.

I ask him all the time, "What's your name, boy?"

"Tim Brown," he'll say.

"That's right. Don't you ever forget that. That's a special name." Sometimes I add, "And remember, when I'm not here, you need to take care of things. You're the man of the house." You can see Timothy's back straighten and his chest stick out a little more when I tell him that.

I've gotten in trouble for that one, though. I was traveling recently, and my wife asked me over the phone, "Tim, what did you say to your son? I'm trying to get him to bed, and he's lying on your side of the bed telling me, 'I'm the man of the house.'"

The story is funny, but it also shows how serious boys are about taking on the role of a man. When they're young, Dad is their hero, and they want to be just like him. As they get older, they start to figure out that Dad has good qualities and some that might not be so good. But they're still watching and listening every second. Their concept of manhood begins with Dad. Sure, they'll do plenty of tinkering as they grow up, but more than anything or anyone else, he's the model they start with and stay with.

That's definitely how it was for me. My father had a huge influence on me. In all my years of living in the same house, I never saw him miss a day of work. Other than summer vacation time, he never took a day off, not even for being sick. It was his job to be there, and he always showed up. I know that example helped drive me when I got to the NFL. It's why over seventeen years I missed only one practice, and that was for my dad's heart surgery. My mind-set was, *My job is to be at practice. I need to get this done. It's what a man does.*

That came from my dad.

I also watched my father come home every night. Sure, he was always out late managing the nightclub. But no matter how good or bad a day he had, no matter how he felt about his wife or his kids on a particular evening, we knew he was coming home. There was no running around. We knew that if somebody tried to break into our house in the middle of the night, Daddy would be there defending us. We could count on him.

That's also what a man does. He's consistent. He protects and takes care of his family.

The truth is that even though there were a few rough spots, my upbringing was just about perfect for me. I learned so much about what it means to be a man by watching my dad. His relationship with God? That was another matter. I had to filter everything he said and did through the realization that he didn't have a spiritual foundation. In that area, I'm trying to give my kids a different example.

Of course, so many men and boys today didn't or don't have any example to follow. Their father was or is either absent altogether or someone whose life has been about poor choices, lack of responsibility, and no understanding of the meaning of manhood. If you're that man or boy, or if you're reading this as a mom whose son doesn't have a real man in his life, I strongly encourage you to get with someone who had or has a good father and is one today. It might be an older man or someone your own age. Either way, don't be embarrassed to seek help and advice. Ask him, "What is being a good dad all about?" He may even be able to step in himself and spend time with you or your son.

You can only get so much from a book. You've got to connect with those who've seen it and lived it. They can teach you what you need to know.

Too many sons, and daughters too, are growing up today without a dad or true father figure. The statistics on fatherless families seem to get worse every year. It's a national tragedy. Boys need their fathers in order to discover what manhood is all about. We need to do all we can to support and guide these soon-to-be men, especially if we're dads ourselves.

It's what a man does.

4

A MAN USES
HIS SKILLS

As each has received a gift, use it to serve one another.

1 PETER 4:10 ESV

O ut of the 'hood and onto the hill. For me, life was pretty good when our family moved from the little fourplex in South Dallas to our two-bedroom house on a hill in East Dallas. It was a much better neighborhood, not high class by any means, but an area where a kid could roam around until nine in the evening, or even ten in the summer, without anyone worrying about it.

I was entering second grade and made a bunch of new friends, both in the neighborhood and at Mount Auburn Elementary. We did all kinds of things together—bicycle races, improvised games, bicycle jumps on ramps we built ourselves. Those ramps never held up very well. Whoever was brave enough to go first often ended up getting slammed in the face by a board. One of my new friends,

Mike Alexander, had the first video game I'd ever seen, Atari's Pong. No kid today would waste his time on something so basic, but we used to play that thing for hours.

Our walk to school every morning was more than two miles, which we did in all kinds of weather. We went down the street and across the bridge over Interstate 30, cut through Tenison Park, walked by the swimming pool and Samuel Recreation Center where I spent so much time in the summer, and then down a long street. We had the routine down.

At Mount Auburn, I acquired the typical skills in reading, writing, and 'rithmetic. But the most important lesson I learned might have been on the playground grass. We didn't play organized team sports. It was all just messing around. But the first time someone tossed me a football and everyone started chasing me, I found out that I was faster and had better moves than most of the kids. They couldn't tackle me.

It was a little scary to have everyone trying to get me, but it was fun too—especially since they couldn't catch me.

My brother, Wayne, was actually the one who sparked my interest in football. Before we moved, he'd been a high school running back at Samuel High School—a good one. He and my dad always watched the Cowboys on TV, so I started joining in and picked up nuances of the game from both of them.

Wayne liked to take me out in the yard and throw a football at me. Not with me, but *at* me. He decided he needed to toughen me up, so he fired that ball as hard as he could at his little eight-year-old brother to see if I could catch it. It was torture at the time, but the more we did that, the better I developed what he called "soft hands." Within two or three years, I started catching those fireballs. Wayne seemed to lose interest in our football sessions after that.

In sixth grade, the principal at Mount Auburn said he had been watching me and thought I was an athlete with exceptional hand-eye coordination. He wanted to teach me how to play golf, but I didn't take him up on it. At eleven years old, I didn't think of myself as an athlete, and learning how to swing a golf club sounded like the craziest idea I'd ever heard.

Then for seventh grade I entered J. L. Long Middle School and played on my first football team. I was never a big guy, but always just a little faster than the rest. I soon realized that what I'd discovered in grade school was still true—when people came at me, I had a natural ability to make them miss. The coaches noticed that too. They loved watching me return punts and kickoffs, and started getting me the ball on plays from scrimmage as well. We watched films of our games—in Texas, even middle school football is serious business—and when I saw myself easily eluding guys on the other team, it gave me more confidence.

I still remember a play from one of our early home games. Seventh graders don't have great throwing arms, so we didn't pass very often, but we did on this play. I caught a short pass from our quarterback and ran laterally. A guy was trying to catch me from behind and another opponent was coming straight at me to make the tackle. I did a little dip with my head to fake the defender in front of me, and these two guys crashed into each other while I scored a touchdown. It was like something you'd see on a cartoon.

Later, when we watched that play on film, our coach said, "Tim, that was pretty nice." It got me thinking that I could do something special out there. *When you run like that, those guys can't touch you,* I told myself. *You keep doing that and see how that works for you.*

———

I also played basketball and ran track in middle school. I did more of the same when I moved across the campus from J. L. Long to

Woodrow Wilson High School. I was pretty good as a point guard for the Wildcats, earning all-district and state honorable mention honors. In track, my events were the 400 meter the 4 x 100 meter relay, the mile relay, and the long jump. I lettered in track all four years of high school and qualified for regionals in the 400 and long jump my senior year. Sports just seemed to come easy for me.

Athletics weren't my only interest, however. I loved math and English, which some of my friends thought was weird, and I was also intrigued by a field that seemed to have a bright future: computers. I became sports editor of the school newspaper. My freshman year, I even played bass drum in the marching band.

My dad was still making comments such as "When you end up in jail, don't call me," so I was more determined than ever to show him how wrong he was about me. I studied hard and my grades were always good. There were times, in fact, when I went up to one of my teachers during class and said, "I finished my assignment early. Can I get more work?"

That probably made me seem even stranger to my friends.

Despite that, and even though I was a quiet kid, I seemed to be popular with my classmates. Woodrow, as we called it, was more than 60 percent white at the time. The white kids lived in the Lakewood area, which was a different stratosphere in terms of economics. Those kids lived in nice homes, often drove cars their parents gave them, and always seemed to have money in their pockets. You could say that the whites and blacks at Woodrow lived in two different worlds, but it wasn't a tense situation at all. Even though my dad was often saying things like "You don't want to work for the white man," I seemed to get along with them better than most of my friends. I never looked at white kids as different, and they never treated me as different.

That, along with my success as an athlete, probably had something to do with me being voted vice president of my senior class. I was also voted most likely to succeed and best looking (don't know how to explain that one). Overall, my high school experience was great.

———

There was one other interest that captured my attention during high school, and for better or for worse, it would be a recurring theme in the years to come.

I discovered girls.

By the time I was sixteen, I was head over heels for a pretty, funny, popular girl I'll call "Christy." She lived only a couple of blocks away, and I spent as much time with her as I could. During the school year, my routine was the same on Mondays, Tuesdays, and Thursdays, the evenings we didn't go to church. After classes I had practice for whatever sport was in season, followed by dinner by myself at home, which was usually whatever my family hadn't finished earlier in the evening. (I like dark meat today because I developed a taste for it as a teenager—dark chicken meat was usually all that was left for me to eat.) Dinner was followed by a homework session. Then I was off to Christy's.

If I wasn't with Christy, I was usually hanging out with my good friend Harold Saunders. On the weekends, Christy, Harold, his girl-friend, and I often went out together—dances, movies, whatever. We had a lot of fun together.

I should probably credit Christy for developing the sprinting ability I showed on the athletic fields. My weeknight curfew was 10:00 p.m., and I always stretched it to the limit when I was with her. As soon as my watch said 9:50, I was out the door.

That first street was not at all well lit—it was almost totally dark. Between my fear of whatever was out there in the night and my fear of Dad's reaction if I got home late, I was motivated to move! I would get into the middle of the street and run wide open that first hundred yards. I booked it every time, scared for my life.

I learned a lot in high school, not only about what my teachers were trying to get across but also about myself and what that might mean for my future. During my first year on the Woodrow football team, the *Dallas Morning News* did a story about me and other standout high school players with the headline "Sophomore Sensations." I was from a family of athletes, so my sports achievements weren't a big deal at home. Besides Wayne's success in football, Ann was all-district in track and eventually became a college All-American in volleyball, while Gwen was all-district in volleyball. But that headline got me thinking about possibilities down the road. Maybe my ability as an athlete could help me get a college education.

People were starting to tell me that I had amazing talent, but I didn't want it to go to my head. I knew better than to take credit for it. I understood because of what I'd been taught at church: God had given me a gift.

Some might wonder why God would bless someone with athletic ability or if He expects us to use that ability. They might ask how playing football, for example, does anything to help others or advance God's purposes. Some in my church, as a matter of fact, were asking that question as my football career developed. Not openly, but I could hear the whispers that I was wasting my time or, worse, I couldn't play football and belong to God at the same time.

That was hard for me to hear, and I know those kinds of comments can be discouraging for any young man trying to figure out his place in life. Sooner or later, most of us start asking ourselves,

"What are my skills? How am I supposed to use them? What does God want me to do with my life?"

For me, the key to answering those questions is having a spiritual connection to God. When you're in tune with Him, reading His words in the Bible and praying, you're in a position to get the answers you need. Go ahead and ask Him to give you the gifts He has in mind for you and to make it obvious what they are. They may not be the talents that others have, but that's okay. We're not all born to be preachers or missionaries or musicians at the front of the church. Maybe you're skilled at repairing cars or balancing a budget. Each of us is unique and each of us has a place in God's plan.

In my case, though I might not have been able to put it into words at the time, I sensed that God had a purpose for the athletic ability He'd given me. I didn't know what that purpose was, but I didn't question the direction He seemed to be pointing. I believed that somehow there would be a way for me to use my talent to serve others and bring glory to Him.

I've also come to realize that athleticism isn't my only talent. What was true for me in high school when I was around the white kids has remained true during the rest of my life: I have the ability to be comfortable and relate well with people from all walks of life. As I deal with men and women in the sports world, in entertainment, in business, and in the spiritual community, that's been a tremendous asset. Again, I know it isn't anything I've done. It's a gift God has given me, and I'm tremendously grateful for it.

Your gifts are probably entirely different from mine—the ability to listen well, to multitask, to find solutions to complex problems, to work with children or machines, encouragement, empathy. Whatever they are, ask God to reveal them to you, and don't be afraid to embrace them. He's given them to you for a reason, even if you can't see it right now. I believe that if we use the talents God gives us to the best of our abilities and dedicate our efforts to Him, He'll be pleased with the results.

———————

We had winning seasons when I played football and basketball in middle school, but that wasn't the case at Woodrow. In our best football season while I was there, we won just two games. We had a few decent players—including tackle Lionel Douglas, quarterback Benny Tovar, and running and defensive backs Vincent Pride and Monty Martin—just not enough of them. Other schools had much more depth.

On the football field, my hero was Eric Dickerson, an All-American running back for Southern Methodist University when I was a sophomore. He wore a protective device we called a neck roll, so I started wearing one too. I even tried to lift my knees like he did when I got in the open field. And since he was a running back, that was my preferred position too—although the coaches also used me as a quarterback, receiver, and kick returner. It seemed like I never lined up in the same spot for two consecutive plays. Not until my senior year did I start playing more at receiver. I realized I didn't have a running back's mentality. Their approach is to look for four yards, break tackles, and then try to turn it into forty yards. I just wanted to bounce outside and get away. I was always looking for the forty.

Our basketball team didn't fare much better than the football team. We'd hang in against most teams until the third quarter, then they'd start to pull away. Once that happened, my goal became to make a steal or run ahead on a fast break so I could throw down a dunk. I was a pretty good defender and actually considered myself better on the court than on the gridiron. I dreamed of getting attention from a top basketball program like Duke or North Carolina.

That's not what happened, though. My life changed during a Thursday night football game during my junior year. Our opponent was Skyline High, the one school we beat every season. I had a big game, scoring touchdowns on a kickoff return, a punt return, a long pass, and a long run from scrimmage.

What I didn't know was that a Notre Dame coach, Jay Robertson, was in the stands to scout Skyline's star linebacker Dante Jones. (Dante went on to an eight-year NFL career himself, mostly with the Chicago Bears. Today he lives around the corner from me. Every time I see him, I say, "Thank you, brother.")

The morning after the game, Coach Robertson was waiting for Richard Mason, our head coach, when he arrived at work. "Who's this Tim Brown kid," Robertson said, "and why do I not know anything about him?"

Before that night, no one in the world of college football knew who I was. But the next week, I started getting letters of interest from programs across the country, including Notre Dame.

My brother was a huge fan of Fighting Irish football. He used to get up early every Sunday morning to watch the television replay of the Notre Dame game from the day before. Wayne came over that week when I had my letters spread out across the kitchen table. He picked up the one from Notre Dame and read it.

"If they still want him a year from now," he said to my mom, "this is where he needs to go."

I wasn't so sure. Call me naïve, but I really hadn't even thought about playing college football. My goal up to that point had been to study at a local junior college for a couple of years, finish up at a nearby four-year school, and then get a job. Suddenly it looked like football might actually pay for my education, which was mind blowing. But leave home? I wasn't on board with that idea yet. You have to remember how close I was to my family. I hadn't been away from them before, not even for a single night. I was *not* excited about moving to another state, even to go to college and play football.

The coaches were excited about me, though. Some of the biggest names in the sport showed up in our living room: Tom Osborne from Nebraska, Barry Switzer from Oklahoma, Hayden Fry from Iowa, Jackie Sherrill from Texas A&M, and yes, Gerry Faust from Notre Dame. There were plenty more. No one could officially offer me a scholarship until I completed my high school football eligibility during my senior season, but their intentions were clear.

Sometimes the offers were for more than a scholarship. I heard about a new house for my parents, a new job for my dad, a college scholarship for Christy, and cars, jewelry, and cash for me, starting at $1,250 a month. That all sounded pretty tempting to a seventeen-year-old. If this was how these things worked, I was open to talking about it, especially if it would help my family. But my parents wouldn't touch any of that. They wanted nothing under the table. They just wanted me to get a good education.

For a long time, I was leaning toward SMU. They had a great football team and strong academic program, and the campus was only five miles from my house. But then the whispers started about potential NCAA infractions (the NCAA eventually handed the "death penalty" to SMU, terminating the football program for the 1987 season). My parents and Wayne, meanwhile, favored Notre Dame.

Coach Faust visited during the summer before my senior year. My dad was at work, so it was me, Mama, and Wayne with him in the living room. The Notre Dame approach was different. Nothing was said about cash or extra benefits. The emphasis was on academics and how 99 percent of Notre Dame athletes graduated.

My mother surprised me in that meeting. I hadn't played bass drum in the band since my freshman year, but I discovered she still had a secret desire for me to revert back to my modest music career. She asked, "Is it possible for my son to get a band scholarship?"

I have to give credit to Coach Faust. He didn't even crack a smile. Instead, he said, "No, I'm sorry, Mrs. Brown, we can't give Tim a band scholarship. But if he comes to Notre Dame and practices even one day with the team, and then decides he doesn't want to play football, he'll still have a scholarship." That sounded pretty good to my mom. It was the only time we heard that from a school.

Following my senior football season, with my future still up in the air, I visited the Notre Dame campus for the first time. It was January 20, 1984. A recent snowfall had layered everything in a blanket of white. I turned up Notre Dame Avenue and viewed the famous Golden Dome that capped the main administration building. Sunshine glinted off the gilded dome and stately statue of Mary at its peak.

Wow—the picturesque scene took my breath away.

At that moment, I knew. Over. Done. I was joining the Fighting Irish.

5

PERSISTENCE CREATES CONFIDENCE

Whether you think you can or think you can't—you are right.

HENRY FORD

Knute Rockne, the Four Horsemen, and "Win one for the Gipper."
Frank Leahy. Ara Parseghian. Twelve national championships.
Six Heisman Trophies. Touchdown Jesus. The Fighting Irish of
Notre Dame represented the most storied program in college foot-
ball. Incredibly, I was now part of it.

And I wanted to go home.

Like everyone on the team, I'd arrived on campus in July, before
classes, to begin practice for the upcoming season. Unlike the rest of
my new teammates, I'd brought most of my family with me. Mama,
Wayne and his wife, Gwen and her husband, my nieces Karina and
Tosha, my new sister Kathy, only two at the time, and even my girlfriend, Christy, stayed in a South Bend, Indiana, hotel for nearly a

week. I spent every lunch and dinner break with them instead of with the other players.

Then my family went back to Texas.

It hit me in the middle of practice just hours after they'd left— my family, my support system, was *gone*. I wouldn't see them for another six to eight weeks. I was surrounded by a hundred guys who knew what they were doing. I didn't know these guys and I did *not* know what I was doing. I had just turned eighteen years old, and I was alone.

Suddenly I couldn't think or function. I didn't hear the plays being called in the huddle and didn't hear what the coaches were telling me. For the next three days, I walked around in a daze. I looked like a zombie and felt like a lost sheep. Everything in me was saying, "Leave. Go. You want to be with your family? Just get on a plane and go home."

Fortunately, I didn't do that. I have to give some of the credit to Alvin Miller, a teammate who became a good friend. Back for his second year at Notre Dame, Alvin was also a receiver and also from a big, close family. He took me under his wing and said, "Dude, it's going to be rough for a little while and you're going to feel lonely. But it's going to be all right."

The biggest thing that happened during those three days, though, is that I simply grew up. I started thinking, *You've got a great opportunity here. Do you think Mama or Daddy wants to see you come home a failure? You can't go home like that. It's time to man up, beat on your chest like Tarzan, and deal with it.*

By the end of two weeks, things started to click and I knew I was going to make it. I'd complained on earlier phone calls home, but now my attitude was completely different. "You all right?" Mama asked.

"Oh, yeah," I said. "I'm fine."

If there was any doubt, I knew for certain I wasn't in high school anymore when I looked at some of my new teammates. At Woodrow, our linemen were about the same size as me, six feet and 170 pounds. Notre Dame's offensive line, meanwhile, was the biggest in football, college *or* pros. These guys were each about six feet five inches and looked about 330 pounds. When I first saw them, I thought, *What the heck is going on here?*

I had another adjustment to make when I walked onto the Astroturf in Indianapolis for our first game of the season. I'd never played in front of more than four hundred people during my high school career. We'd have the band, a few family members, and some other fans scattered across the bleachers, and that was it. Now we were opening against Purdue in the first game ever played in the new Hoosier Dome (later renamed the RCA Dome), which sat more than sixty thousand people. The game was sold out.

Coach Faust knew I hadn't played in front of a big crowd before. He wanted me to be the team's kickoff and punt returner, but he also said he wanted to "work me in slowly." We were ranked No. 7 in the Associated Press preseason poll, so the expectations and pressure were high. Working in slowly sounded like a good plan to me.

Which is why I was shocked when seconds before we lined up to leave the locker room and take the field for the game, Coach Faust suddenly looked for me and yelled, "Tim Brown! If we win the kick-off, I want you to return it."

I was so stunned that I left my helmet in the locker room. A teammate had to tell me, "Tim, you'd better go back and get that." Mentally, I was out of it. On the sideline, I begged, *Please, God, let us lose the opening coin toss.*

We won it, of course, and elected to receive. I ran onto the field and gave myself a quick pep talk: "Tim, this is football. Catch the ball and run with it. It's not hard."

Purdue kicked off. It was a squib kick that bounced all over the place. To my relief, I was able to scoop it up, but by the time I did the Purdue coverage team was almost on top of me. I took two steps, ran into one of my teammates, and took two more steps before I realized I didn't have the ball. The collision with my teammate had knocked it out of my hands.

I turned to try to recover the fumble, but it was too late. Purdue had the ball on our eight yard line and soon kicked a field goal.

So much for impressing the world in my college football debut. After the fumble, Joe Johnson, a strong safety and one of our senior captains, stopped me as I ran off the field and he went on. "Son," he said, "you're going to have to be one heck of a football player or they're going to run you out of here."

The football staff had already seen enough of me for that game. One coach said, "Stay near me. We'll let you know when we want you to go back in." I was devastated. I couldn't have drawn up a less inspiring start to my career at Notre Dame.

It was late in the Purdue game, with us trailing and needing to score, when I heard the coaches call for our three-receiver package. During the previous two weeks of practice I'd been that third receiver, so without thinking I grabbed my helmet and ran onto the field. I'd covered about three-quarters of the distance to the huddle when I realized, *Wait, I'm not supposed to be out here.* But I didn't stop. *I'm not turning around. I've got to make up for that fumble.*

The play called for me to run across the middle. I didn't expect the pass to come my way, but I turned out to be the open man. Steve Beuerlein's throw was high and a little behind me, a tough catch even without the pressure of a tight game. But this time I came through. I reached back and was just able to close my fingers around it. We gained nineteen yards and got a first down that led to a score.

The coaches didn't let me back in the game after that play, but I'd made my mark. For me, that catch meant everything. It was probably the most important play of my college career. The kickoff fumble had already raised doubts about my mental toughness with the coaches and my teammates, and maybe even in my own mind. If I'd dropped the pass too, I certainly would have gone into the next week questioning myself. Crazy as it sounds, I might have been a different player from that point. But in that moment when I was running onto the field and had to decide if I would keep going to the huddle or return to the sideline, I *knew* I had to try. I wanted to play. I wanted to prove I belonged. If the coaches weren't yet ready to give me a second chance, I needed to create one.

The catch against Purdue solidified in my mind that I could play this game at the college level. Later, after I joined the Raiders, owner Al Davis often said, "I don't like it when Tim makes a mistake or has a bad game. But I know if he does, the next opportunity he has to correct it, he will." That determined, positive attitude started with my first catch from Beuerlein in the Hoosier Dome.

Even though we scored on that drive, it wasn't enough for us to come all the way back. We lost the Purdue game, 23–21, and fell out of the national rankings. In many ways it reflected our season—we showed a lot of promise at times, but often couldn't finish the way we wanted.

The Purdue loss was followed by three straight wins, and then three losses. I started feeling more comfortable and played better in the second half of the season, and the team played better too. We were 3–4 when we knocked off seventh-ranked Louisiana State at Tiger Stadium, 30–22. We followed that victory with wins over Navy, 18–17; Penn State, 44–7; and the University of

Southern California, 19–7. USC was ranked No. 14 coming into that game. It was played in a driving Los Angeles rain, making for a slippery ball; the Trojans fumbled eight times. I scored my first touchdown for the Irish in that game, an eleven-yard shovel pass from Beuerlein.

The win earned us a No. 17 ranking and a spot in the Aloha Bowl in Honolulu against SMU, the school I'd originally hoped to play for. Unfortunately, we didn't show them that I'd made the better choice. John Carney kicked a field goal late in the game to pull us within 27–20. We got the ball back and drove to the SMU sixteen yard line. But with thirty seconds to go, on fourth down, Beuerlein overthrew an open Milt Jackson in the end zone. That was the game.

I had one catch on the day, for sixteen yards.

For me, it wasn't a bad season. I caught twenty-eight passes, a Notre Dame freshman record, for 340 yards. I also averaged 17.3 yards on seven kickoff returns. But I felt the way I believe the team felt—it could have been more.

———

When you think of the weather in Dallas, you think hot. Sometimes dry, sometimes humid, but always hot. The temperature hardly ever drops below freezing. So for me, that first winter at Notre Dame was brutal. We're not talking about inches of snow; we're talking feet.

I remember when the first big snow hit. I looked out the window of my dorm room the next morning, saw everything covered in white, and said to myself, "Oh, man, I'm not going to class today." My roommate was Brandy Wells, a defensive back from New Jersey. Before I could even suggest a plan for the day, Brandy said, "Hey, I gotta go to class." He was out the door.

I called Alvin Miller. "Hey man, want to go over to the student union, get some hamburgers, and hang out?"

"Yeah, Timmy, that sounds like a good idea," he said. "Let's do that, but let me go to class first. Then I'll meet you over there."

I called a couple more of the boys and got the same answer. *Hold on*, I thought. *I'm not going to be the only one* not *going to class*. It was peer pressure in a good way. That's how it was at Notre Dame. People weren't there to mess around. They were there to get something done.

Did we have fun too? Yes. Did we do weird, crazy things sometimes? Yes again. There was the night we had a jeans-ripping party. If you showed up at the party with jeans on, we ripped your pockets off. Sure it was dumb—and a problem if you owned only one pair of jeans—but we had a blast.

For me, Notre Dame was the right place at the right time. I was still young and impressionable enough that if I'd gone to a party school, I could have ended up in all kinds of trouble, despite my solid upbringing. I definitely hoped to enjoy my college years, but I also wanted that degree so I could get a job and support a family someday. I saw that as part of the Notre Dame community, I could have all of that if I was willing to work for it.

I just hoped I could also contribute enough on the football field to justify my scholarship.

———

The 1985 season was the fifth and final year of Gerry Faust's contract at Notre Dame. Coach Faust had been hired after leading one of the most successful high school programs in the country, Moeller High in Cincinnati, where his teams won four national titles. After four mostly so-so seasons in South Bend, his 1985 team began the year ranked No. 13 in the AP poll. Hopes were high that we'd turn things around.

Unfortunately, that isn't what happened. Michigan upset us in the opener, 20–12. We came back the next week to defeat Michigan State, 27–10, in a game where I returned a kickoff ninety-three yards for a touchdown. But two losses followed.

Going into the second-to-last game of the season, our record was 5-4. We hosted Louisiana State in what turned out to be a defensive battle. On our first drive, I scored on a trick play, an eighteen-yard end around. That one touchdown was still enough for a 7–3 lead in the fourth quarter, but LSU punched in a score with a little over three minutes left. We had a chance to retake the lead, but I let a critical pass slip through my fingers. The play called for me to run deep, then cut into the middle for what would have been a twenty-yard gain. It wouldn't have been an easy play to make, but the pass was catchable.

LSU hung on to win, 10–7. It was an awful feeling walking off the field that day.

Coach Faust must have known what was coming. He resigned during the following week, effective at the end of the season. In the final game, fourth-ranked Miami destroyed us, 58–7.

Gerry Faust is one of the greatest guys I've ever met. He's a nice man, energetic, encouraging, who loves Notre Dame and the Catholic faith. Some said that he was in over his head at Notre Dame, that as a former high school coach he wasn't prepared for all the demands of major college football. I don't know if I can judge that. At the time, I was just trying to fit in. I know he was doing the best he could and that he was disappointed that the results weren't better.

I was disappointed personally as well. My twenty-five catches were down from the season before, although it was enough to lead the team and my average yards per catch went up. I also led the team with fourteen kickoff returns for 338 yards and scored five touchdowns overall. Again, I felt capable of much more.

What really got me was my hunch that the coaches didn't believe in me. I wondered if I didn't play as much as I could have because they felt I was no good under pressure. From my performance, I could understand that thinking to some degree. I just felt that they hadn't yet seen the real Tim Brown.

———

Lou Holtz, who'd led Minnesota to the Independence Bowl the previous year, was hired as the new Notre Dame coach. He was different than any coach I'd been around. He was so sure of himself and his approach that you couldn't help wanting to hear what he had to say. One of the first changes he announced was that our jerseys would no longer show our last names. He wanted to emphasize that we were a team.

I met and got to know Coach Holtz a little during our 5:30 a.m. winter workouts. But on just the second day of spring practice, he pulled me out of a wide receivers drill and called me over.

This couldn't be good. I wondered what I'd done wrong.

"Son, tell me the story," he said.

"What story?" I asked.

"The story."

I didn't know what he was talking about. "Coach, what story?"

"Was it grades? Discipline issues? Why weren't you playing more?"

I didn't know what to say because I didn't know for sure. "Coach, there's no answer. They just didn't play me."

"Don't lie to me," he said, his voice rising. "There's no coaching staff in America dumb enough to not play you!"

After a few more questions, Coach Holtz finally seemed convinced that I hadn't been held out because of a conspiracy or anything sinister on my part. Then he really surprised me.

"Son," he said, "unless the other team intercepts the snap from center, you will get the ball. You could be the best player in the country."

That sounded like crazy talk to me. As far as I was concerned, I wasn't even the best player on our team. I decided our new coach knew I was fairly popular with the players and was trying to make some friends on the team. He just wanted me on his side.

But Lou Holtz didn't stop with that statement. He pulled me aside every day to talk about my ability and my potential. He repeatedly had me watch film of myself to remind me of what I'd already done when I had the chance. After two weeks of his consistent attention and positive message, I began to think, *Hey, maybe I can do something big here.*

For the first time since I'd come to Notre Dame, I started to truly believe in myself. I kept listening to Coach Holtz, watching film, and working hard in practice. By the end of that spring, I believed no one could touch me on the football field.

Confidence is critical to success in life. An athlete can have incredible talent, but it's the mind that tells the body what to do. When you're playing in a stadium filled with eighty thousand people, with millions more watching on television, talent isn't enough. You have to be mentally strong or the pressure will get to you. A little self-confidence shortage will suddenly turn into a big problem.

Some guys are born with overflowing assurance, but the rest of us have to cultivate it. So how does a man develop confidence?

By being *persistent.* We must persistently work on our skills in our chosen profession. We have to persistently maintain and improve our important relationships. We must persistently seek to be the best friends, husbands, and fathers we can. If we're people of faith, we need to persistently pursue God. Halfhearted, temporary efforts won't cut it. Deep down, we'll know we haven't given it our all. When the pressure's on, we won't have the confidence we need to carry us through.

Right now I'm the assistant coach for my daughter Timon's high school track team. Too often, when I ask these kids to do something that challenges them, such as adding an extra event before a meet, the answer I get is, "My body won't hold up. I can't do it."

"Why," I say, "are you telling me what you can't do before you even try? If you go out there and fail, then we'll know you can't do it. But don't tell me you can't do something without even trying."

Sometimes those with the most natural ability are the ones who have the hardest time. They expect things to come easily, which is probably the case at first. But the higher the level, the greater the challenge. They soon discover that persistent effort is the only way to improve and develop confidence. It's hard, but it works.

I had plenty of chances to sabotage my football career at Notre Dame. I could have gone home that first week after my family left. I could have turned around and gone back to the sidelines on my first play after my fumble against Purdue. I could have given up during my first two years when the coaches didn't believe in me enough to play me regularly. Yet I persisted. It wasn't any great achievement on my part and it didn't lead to noticeable results right away. But it put me in position to grow the confidence I needed when Coach Holtz saw my potential.

That spring was about a mind-set change. I wasn't any bigger, faster, or stronger than before, but I was *playing* bigger, faster, and stronger. I'd come to believe, "I'm the best out there. Let me just go do what I do."

––––––––––

The first test of the new Tim Brown came in our 1986 season opener against Michigan. We were the unranked home team, while Michigan was ranked No. 3 in the country. The game was a sellout, as usual at Notre Dame, but interest and enthusiasm were off the charts. People wondered what this new coach and new team could do.

I quickly discovered that Coach Holtz wasn't kidding about getting me the ball. It was a little like high school again, in that I was all over the field. We ran a wishbone offense, and I lined up at different times as wide receiver, flanker, and running back. I rushed twelve times for sixty-five yards, the most I ever carried the ball in college. One of those carries was a three-yard touchdown. I also caught a thirty-two-yard pass and returned a kickoff.

Michigan couldn't stop us that day. We rolled up 455 yards of total offense and never punted. Unfortunately, we stopped ourselves with three turnovers inside the Wolverines' twenty yard line. When John Carney missed a forty-five-yard field goal attempt at the end of the game, Michigan escaped with a 24–23 win. Yet the fans gave us a standing ovation anyway. There was a feeling that times had changed.

They certainly had for me. As the season wore on, my play improved. Against Air Force, I ran a kickoff back ninety-five yards for a touchdown. The week after, I made seven catches for 184 yards and a touchdown against Navy. The following week, the team and I got some revenge against SMU. I had four catches for 176 yards and a touchdown, and we rolled over the Mustangs, 61–29.

When the season started, I already believed in what Coach Holtz had been telling me. Now my play confirmed it. I'd changed from a guy who was shaky under pressure into someone who felt that every time the ball came my way, I had the opportunity to do something special. My thinking was, *What can't I do?*

Our team record was 4-6 going into the season finale against seventeenth-ranked USC in the Los Angeles Coliseum. It turned out to be one of the best games of my college career. We were down 30–12 in the third quarter and looked finished, but we didn't give up. I caught a kickoff on our five yard line and returned it up the left hash mark for fifty-seven yards. We scored a few plays later and added a two-point conversion to get within 30–20. USC answered with a touchdown to take a 37–20 lead with a little over twelve minutes left, but we came back again on a forty-seven-yard touchdown pass from Beuerlein to Milt Jackson. USC 37, Notre Dame 27.

USC then nearly drove the length of the field, but on fourth down on our five yard line, our defense stopped Rodney Peete's quarterback keeper inches short of a first down. We had the ball with six minutes left. I was able to make another big play, catching a forty-nine-yard bomb from Beuerline along the right sideline. Braxston Banks scored on a pass around the left end, Beuerline connected on another two-point pass, and we were down just 37–35.

Our defense stopped the Trojans again. At this point, I was one of the nation's leading kickoff returners. During a timeout, as USC faced fourth down, a coach told us, "They're probably not going to kick to Tim. Let's go for a half-line block. If they miskick the ball, the other guys can give Tim a shot to return it."

I fully expected the kick to go to the sideline. When that ball floated my direction, I was surprised and nervous, thinking, *The ball! The ball's coming!*

I caught it on our twenty-eight yard line, ran right, and slipped away from a Trojan who got a hand on me. I turned on the after-burners near midfield and outran two more defenders. Another player hit me at the USC twenty-two, but I pulled away from him before somebody finally brought me down at the sixteen. When I got up, there was a lot of helmet slapping and cheering. The team and the Notre Dame fans in the Coliseum were fired up. It was a fifty-six-yard return, and we still had a little over two minutes to play.

We worked the clock. On our last shot at the end zone, I carried from the six to the two yard line, but didn't have enough room to get in. With two seconds left, John Carney lined up for a nineteen-yard field goal. He'd missed a couple in recent weeks, but this one was perfect, giving us the 38–37 victory in front of the stunned crowd. I'd gained 254 all-purpose yards.

We were celebrating in the locker room when Jim Murray, the Pulitzer Prize–winning sports columnist for the *Los Angeles Times*, came up to me and said, "You're going to be my frontrunner for the Heisman next year." I couldn't believe it.

Most of our family was with me for the game. When I left the locker room, I told my brother what Jim Murray had said. Wayne looked at me. I looked at him. Then we both burst out laughing. It felt too crazy and too good to be true. A few minutes later, I said to Wayne, "Hey bro, even if I don't win the Heisman, do you think somebody might want me to play in the NFL?" We both cracked up again. It just didn't seem real.

But it was. Thanks to a little persistence, a new level of confidence, and God's blessing, I was suddenly looking at opportunities I hadn't even dreamed of.

6

MEN NEED MENTORS

Young kids with positive male role models have
something to live for, somebody who is proud of them,
somebody who cares about their well-being.

DONALD MILLER

The majority of the college football preseason publications had me as their Heisman Trophy frontrunner for 1987. Notre Dame even pitched in by creating "Heisman Hankies" that were mailed to the media. What most got people's attention, however, was *Sports Illustrated*. The magazine editors put me on the August 31 cover along with the headlines "Notre Dame's Mr. T" and "Tim Brown: Best Player in the Land." It was pretty heady stuff for a guy who not too long before hadn't even thought about playing college football.

The funny thing was that *Sports Illustrated* was (and still is) famous for having a cover jinx—if you appeared on the cover, bad things were supposed to be around the corner. Plenty of guys on the team said to me, "You can forget about winning the Heisman now."

Which, in a way, is exactly what my teammates and I did. Notre Dame hadn't had a good season for a long time. We knew we had the potential in 1987 to do something special. Everybody else was talking about the Heisman, but in the locker room, it was hardly mentioned. The focus wasn't on winning awards but on winning games, which was just the way I wanted it.

To help us keep our focus in the right place, Coach Holtz called me into his office before the season. Now that I was a senior, I looked forward to the chance of being a team captain. We had only three captains, one each for offense, defense, and special teams. I saw it as a prestigious honor, and since the players voted on the title, it was a sign of their respect. So I was taken aback when Coach Holtz said, "Tim, I don't want you to be a captain this year."

He explained that I was about to get a world of media attention, and as a senior and team leader, I would surely be voted in by the players. But he thought it would be better for the team if someone else was in the position. There would be one more guy who felt especially important to the team and who would have a chance to talk to the media. It would also take some pressure off of me, putting me in a better position to just concentrate on playing well and helping the team.

I wasn't too excited about the idea at first, but the more I thought about it, the more it made sense to me. It was an example of the way Coach Holtz was always looking at what was best for each of his players and for the team as a whole.

We opened against Michigan in front of a hundred thousand fans in Ann Arbor. We were ranked No. 16 and Michigan No. 9. Late in the first quarter, we recovered a fumble in Michigan territory. Three plays later, Terry Andrysiak launched a pass toward me in the left back corner of the end zone. The pass was high, and two other defenders were on me. My confidence was so high at that point, however, that I expected to make the catch. Somehow I jumped a foot higher than the other guys and brought it down for an eleven-yard touchdown. We went on to upset the Wolverines, 26–7. It was a great start to the season.

The media hype only intensified for our next game. Now ranked No. 9, we would face No. 17 Michigan State in our home opener and seventy-second consecutive sellout. The Spartans featured running back Lorenzo White, also a Heisman candidate, so the night contest was billed as a battle of Heisman contenders. It turned out to be the game everyone seems to remember from my college career.

We got a break on the opening kickoff when Michigan State's receiver caught the ball inside the one yard line, took a step back, and downed it. He thought he was already in the end zone, but instead we had a safety and a 2–0 lead. Later in the quarter, we added a field goal. We were up 5–0 when another Spartan drive stalled and they lined up on their forty yard line to punt. Little did I know how big the next few minutes would be for our team and for me.

───────

When I'm waiting for the ball on a punt or kickoff, I don't hear individual voices, but I hear the buzz of the crowd. I've always been pretty good at tuning out the noise around me to concentrate on the task at hand. When I pull the ball in and lock it in place against my forearm—left arm if I'm running left, right arm if I'm running right—the buzz disappears. Everything goes silent except for me thinking, *Time to get this thing done.*

What happens to my ears also happens to my eyes. I'm not seeing the crowd or even the sidelines. It's tunnel vision. If we're set up to return on the right side of the field, I'm looking right for that hole to open up. It's helpful to have good peripheral vision, though, because I do see the guys coming at me from the side.

In that first second or two after I catch the ball, I try to help my blockers by taking a step or making a fake in the opposite direction than I really plan to go. If I can get the other team leaning the wrong way for even a moment, it slows them down as they try to cut back and makes it easier for our blockers to get a good angle on them.

Those blockers are crucial to a successful return. A lot of the guys on Notre Dame special teams were walk-ons, players without a scholarship who loved the game and the Fighting Irish so much that they came out anyway. Kickoffs and punts were usually the only times they played. Without guys like Tom Galloway and Pat Eilers doing their jobs, I'd have been on my back real quick. Nobody would have been talking about Tim Brown's amazing kick returns.

On kickoffs, I didn't want to just catch the ball and start running. When the ball was high in the air, I could tell where it was going to land, so I'd run to within a couple yards of that spot. About two seconds before the ball came down I'd yell, "Go, go, go, go!" That was the signal to my blockers to start running. I did the same thing, running a step or two, so that when I caught the ball I was already cranking up to full speed. The timing had to be just right. I needed to be seven to ten yards behind our wedge of blockers. If they got too far ahead of me, it was easy for the coverage team to go around them and nail me. If the wedge was too close, I'd run into my guys and the blocks wouldn't work.

But we had it down to a science, which is why we were so good on kickoff returns those last couple of years at Notre Dame. In college, and also when I got to the pros, I knew exactly how I wanted us to do it, and the coaches allowed us to do it that way because they understood it would make us more successful.

Punts were a little different in that I was usually alone back there. My punt return technique actually changed under Coach Holtz. Before he arrived, I'd always caught punts with my feet flat on the ground and evenly spaced. But when I dropped a few balls during one of my first spring practices with him, he jumped in to catch a punt and show me what he wanted—feet staggered and arms extended so I could bring the ball in against my body. He actually broke a finger on that catch, but I don't think he cared. He was committed to showing me how to get it right.

On punts, our blockers took their positions along the line of scrimmage and tried to slow down the coverage team from the start. Sometimes we had a specific return called ahead of time that worked just the way it was supposed to. Sometimes I improvised depending on what I saw.

Against Michigan State, it turned out to be a little of both.

I caught the Michigan State punt on our twenty-nine yard line. We had a right return called, so I moved laterally to the right, faked a cut up the middle, and kept going right. Then I turned it up the field and escaped from a couple of guys who tried to bring me down.

I was already past most of the Spartans at this point and running full speed near the sideline. A defender moved toward me at the Notre Dame forty-five yard line. I cut inside to get by him. There was only one Michigan State player left in front of me, and one of my teammates blocked him. Touchdown. The play had worked exactly as designed.

We were up 12–0 and I was out of gas. It was a seventy-one-yard run.

I was still shaking hands and sucking oxygen from a mask on the sideline when our defense stopped Michigan State after just three plays. Somebody came up to me and said, "Tim, it's time to go." I had to be out there for another punt.

I knew how tired I was. I told our special teams coach, George

Stewart, "You guys need to block this. I can't go." So the coach called for a block, with all our guys rushing the kicker and no one running back to help me. My plan, if the punter got the kick off, was to signal a fair catch.

Greg Montgomery was a strong punter for Michigan State, and his kick moved me back several yards to our thirty-four yard line. That gave me more room to do something, so I thought, *Catch the ball and run out of bounds.* I pulled the ball in and ran left, aiming toward the sideline.

But a defender cut me off. I didn't want to do it, but there was a little hole up the middle, so I cut between the guy on my left and two other defenders who both dove and missed me.

Now I was motoring. All my guys who'd gone for the block were running back my way, picking off Michigan State players one by one. It was crazy. Suddenly there was just one man to beat—Montgomery, the punter. Even as exhausted as I was, there was no way I was going to let a punter tackle me. I put a move on him at the twenty and was on my way to the end zone.

I slowed down those last few yards. I had nothing left. In the end zone, I flipped the ball to the ground and one of the guys in the Notre Dame band jumped into my arms. Pretty soon the whole team was jumping on me. I wasn't thinking that we now had a huge lead in the first quarter or that in two minutes I'd returned two punts for touchdowns or that I'd tied an NCAA record for scoring punt returns in a game. All I was thinking was, *I can't breathe.*

We won that game, 31–8, and I gained 275 all-purpose yards. Suddenly everyone seemed to believe the Heisman was mine to lose. I just wanted to keep winning football games.

We did knock off Purdue the next week to go 3-0 and move up to a No. 4 national ranking. But even though I had my best receiving effort of the season in our next game, with six catches for 156 yards, we stumbled against Pittsburgh. We fell behind 27–0 in the first half and saw Terry Andrysiak get knocked out for the rest of the regular season with a broken collarbone. The final score was 30–22.

We got back on track in the next few weeks, defeating Air Force and USC. We also stopped Navy, 56–13. Unfortunately, I also broke the tip of my ring finger in that game. In the first half, I'd moved to block a defensive end and got my hand caught in his jersey, ripping the nail right off. I went to the locker room, and the trainer told me my finger was broken.

I thought I might be done for the day, but the trainer had other ideas. He pulled out a syringe and said, "You might want to look the other way." He stuck that needle into my finger where the nail had been, numbing the pain, and put a splint on it. Then he said, "Get back out there, big boy."

That's when I realized I must be a little crazy to be playing the game of football.

Earlier that season, during a practice, I'd also injured my right shoulder. For the rest of the season, when someone hit me in that spot my shoulder went numb and I had to come out for a few plays. I started wearing extra padding in my shoulder pads, which made me look bigger and heavier than I really was. It bothered me the rest of the year, but we never mentioned it to the media. We didn't want teams targeting my shoulder to try to put me out of the game.

We took a 6-1 record into our game against Boston College and it turned out to be a dogfight. We were down 17–6 at halftime and 25–12 in the third quarter. Tony Rice came off the bench to spark us at quarterback, and Mark Green ran for 133 yards in the second half. He scored the game-winning touchdown with 5:25 left to play.

It was also one of the best games of my college career. On our first play from scrimmage, we ran a play action fake. Even though I was well covered, quarterback Kent Graham hit me in stride and it turned into a fifty-seven-yard gain. On our next drive, I caught three passes for forty-five yards. I had a great day returning kickoffs, finishing with 132 yards on five attempts, and added 126 receiving yards on five catches, 15 rushing yards, and 14 punt return yards. My total of 294 all-purpose yards broke my Notre Dame record.

Our next game, against eleventh-ranked Alabama, was my last at Notre Dame Stadium. After four great years, I didn't want it to end. That day was emotional for me from start to finish. I was the last player introduced to the crowd of almost sixty thousand as I came out of the locker room. I cried on the way to the field, cried during the game, and cried after the game. One former teammate, '86 graduate Dave Butler, pulled me aside just before kickoff and said, "Tim, enjoy the moment. Enjoy all of this, because it will never be again."

If that wasn't enough motivation to play well, there was also the fact that Alabama had stuffed us the year before, 28–10. We definitely wanted to return the favor.

The game was close after the first quarter, 3–3, but then we took over with seventeen consecutive points, eventually winning, 37–6. I had a good day with four catches for 114 yards and 225 all-purpose yards. It was a highly satisfying way to close out my career on campus. Our hopes for a national championship were still alive.

And then came Penn State.

That next Saturday in Beaver Stadium was bitterly cold, with twenty-five-mile-an-hour winds and a wind chill of eight to twenty degrees below zero. For too much of the game, the way we played felt about as cold as the conditions. We fell behind early in the second half, 21–14. Late in the game, however, Tony Rice led us on a sixty-two-yard drive for a touchdown. We were down a point with thirty-one seconds left.

Lou gathered the seniors on the sideline and explained that a tie would take us out of the running for the national title. This was before the days of overtime in college football. He asked us what we wanted to do. It was an easy call. We all said to go for the win.

The conversion play was a quarterback option to the right. Quarterbacks are taught to take it to the end zone if they see an opening, and Tony thought he saw one. I was running with Tony on the play. If he'd faked a run and pitched to me, I would have had an easy path to the end zone. But Tony cut in toward the end zone and a Penn State defender stopped him just short of the goal.

I really don't blame Tony. A team lives and dies on those snap decisions by the quarterback. When I see Tony at different events today, though, I still often say—*mostly* joking—"If only you'd pitched the ball."

The loss to Penn State was a huge disappointment. It locked us into a trip to the Cotton Bowl on New Year's Day, which in a way meant that our final regular-season game against second-ranked Miami didn't matter. That shouldn't have made a difference in our effort. You should always give everything you have when you step onto a football field. But for whatever reason, the team didn't play its best against a very good football team. I turned in the worst performance of my college career, dropping three passes. We lost, 24–0.

———

December 5, 1987, was one of the most nerve-wracking days of my life. I was in New York City's Downtown Athletic Club, waiting for the announcement of the winner of the twenty-five-pound bronze statue known as the Heisman Memorial Trophy Award.

I'd finished 1986 with 1,937 all-purpose yards, a Notre Dame record. I came close to that in 1987, totaling 1,847 all-purpose yards. But my modest finish to the season left some people speculating that it would be a close vote, most likely between me and Syracuse quarterback Don McPherson.

CBS was airing the announcement. Before the ceremony, broadcaster Jim Nantz came up to me and said, "No matter what happens, you've had a good season." *Oh, man,* I thought. *I'm not going to win. If anyone knows, Jim Nantz knows.* A few minutes later, broadcaster James Brown slipped beside me and said, "Hey, you really deserve this award." *Wow,* I thought, *maybe I* did *win it.* I really had no clue, but now that the season and striving for team goals was virtually over, I realized how much I did want to walk away with that trophy.

The time came for us to sit in the front row and hear the results. Five players had been invited to New York: me, McPherson, Lorenzo White, Gordie Lockbaum of Holy Cross, and Craig Heyward of Pittsburgh. I sat somewhere in the middle of those guys. It wasn't as big a production then as it is today. Before I knew it, the club official at the podium was saying, "The fifty-third winner of the Heisman Trophy is . . ." He paused for about two seconds, but it felt like two hours. ". . . Tim Brown of the University of Notre Dame."

I won!

Oh, Lord, I've got to get up and speak.

One of the biggest reasons I was known as a quiet leader in high school and college was that I had a very noticeable lisp. If I didn't have to, I didn't open my mouth. My family never said much about it, and my high school friends didn't make a big deal out of it either. My teammates at Notre Dame were another story. They teased me endlessly by calling me Sylvester, as in Sylvester the Cat from Looney Tunes, by repeating Sylvester's famous "Sufferin' Succotash" line, or by inserting stuffed Sylvester animals in my locker. It wasn't until I reached the pros and a woman I was dating told me a speech therapist could take care of my lisp that I corrected it.

Needless to say, at the Heisman ceremony, I was less than eager to stand in front of America and make a speech. I kept my remarks short and got off the stage. Even so, it was a great moment. From the podium, I could see my mom and dad in the audience. They'd flown up with me for the ceremony, and it was pretty special to think about all they'd done to support me and to know how proud they had to be feeling right then.

Lou Holtz was there too. Even now, I don't have the words to express the impact he had on my life. Before he came to Notre Dame, I'd never even thought about playing football professionally. When a man comes into your life and shows you something about yourself that you didn't know was in you, it's remarkable. The apostle Paul did that for Timothy, encouraging him to preach and teach and reminding him, "Do not neglect your gift" (1 Tim. 4:14). Paul was a mentor to Timothy, ready to point out the gifts of his protégé and willing to help develop those gifts and pass on his knowledge.

Lou Holtz did the same for me, as well as for a whole lot of other guys. That's what a mentor does. I'll always be grateful that he inspired me to believe in myself.

For the last game of my college career, I was coming home. Dallas hosts the Cotton Bowl every year, and back then it was in the stadium named the Cotton Bowl. We were up against Texas A&M, the Southwest Conference champions coached by Jackie Sherrill. There was a lot of talk in the media about the Heisman Trophy winner finishing his career in his hometown. I certainly wanted to play well in front of my family and home fans.

The start was promising. I ran the opening kickoff back thirty-seven yards and finished the drive by catching a seventeen-yard pass from Terry Andrysiak for a touchdown. Early in the second quarter, we added a field goal to take a 10–3 lead. A few minutes later, we were looking for another score, but an Aggie made a leaping interception in front of Andy Heck in the end zone.

From that point on, we couldn't do anything right. I caught six passes for 105 yards in the first half, but none in the second. We gave up the ball three more times on offense and suddenly couldn't seem to stop them on defense.

It got worse. In the third quarter, a Texas A&M player tackled me on a kickoff. Then he grabbed my towel from my belt and ran toward the sideline, waving it like a lasso. I was already frustrated with the way we were playing. Now I was mad. The girlfriend of one of my teammates had gone to the trouble of making and shipping these towels to us before the game. Mine was blue with gold letters that said "Mr. T 81." I wanted that towel back.

I took off after the guy, collared him, wrestled him to the ground, and took my towel back. Was that the best way to handle the situation? Probably not. It earned me a fifteen-yard penalty for unsportsmanlike conduct. It also fired up Texas A&M even more, to the point where it got dangerous for me. They were looking to put me out of the game, and in the fourth quarter one guy did roll my ankle a little bit on the sideline.

Coach Holtz saw that, and noticed I was limping a little after the play. He called me over. "Son," he said, "these guys are trying to end your career. I'm not going to let it happen this way. Just take it in."

I was shocked. "Take it in?" I said.

"Take it in."

I wanted to say, "C'mon, Coach, bring it on. I can handle it." But the game was out of hand. When I thought about it, I realized it made no sense to risk a serious injury, especially now that a career in the pros seemed possible.

We lost the Cotton Bowl, 35–10. It was hardly the finish I'd dreamed of to cap my football legacy at Notre Dame. A lot of guys were pretty upset in the locker room. I was disappointed too, but at the same time, I realized this was still the most successful team I'd ever played on. I was proud of what we'd accomplished and how much the football program had improved. I knew Coach Holtz was the right man to lead Notre Dame in the future—proved the very next year when the Fighting Irish won the national title. Considering the way my football career had taken off thanks to his encouragement and mentorship, he'd certainly been the right man for me. The NFL draft was only a few months away, with everyone saying I'd be an early first-round pick. I couldn't be too unhappy with the way things had turned out.

Besides, I did get my towel back.

Lou Holtz was one of the most influential men in my life at that time, but he wasn't my only mentor. Despite our falling out when I was almost thirteen, my dad was still someone I looked up to in many ways. My brother, Wayne, was in that same category. He was the first person in our family to graduate from college, and he always seemed able to expound on any subject. I used to think, *Man, this guy knows everything.*

There was another man who had and still has a tremendous impact on my life. I think of him as my spiritual mentor. His name is Lafayette Whitley Sr., better known to me as Pastor Whitley of our home church in Dallas.

I've known Pastor Whitley and attended his church since I was twelve. I appreciate his love for and commitment to God and the church. He has always been consistent in his spiritual approach. He preaches from the Bible and doesn't embellish his messages with weird interpretations. He's also always been consistent with me. Whether I was just a teenager or a famous football player, he has treated me the same. That was important to me, especially as my world changed when I moved from high school to college to the pros. I knew my dad wasn't spiritual. I needed a man to be that spiritual rock for me, someone I could count on to always steer me in a godly direction.

It's interesting now to look back on who I was that summer before I left home to start my NFL career. I was almost twenty-two and about to come into a great deal of money. I'd worked hard to get my degree and to earn my status as a sought-after football player. Now the selfish part of me was saying it was time to enjoy myself—girls, cars, maybe whatever else came along.

But at the same time, the spiritually mature part of me was saying I needed to visit my pastor and talk about this. So that's what I did. I sat across from Pastor Whitley in his office at the church. The self-centered part of me wanted to hear, "Tim, go enjoy your life. Have a great time. God understands your heart. I'll catch you in church when you're back home." I secretly wanted his blessing on my plans.

That's not what happened. Instead, Pastor Whitley said, "God has put you on this platform for a reason. It's not to catch footballs. It's for you to bring more people to Him."

Those weren't the words I wanted to hear. I thought, *C'mon, pastor, help a brother out!* Yet that conversation with Pastor Whitley became one of the most important meetings of my life. It set me on a course, and though I took a few detours, it's still the course I aim to follow today.

I've learned that every man needs mentors—people who have gone before you, who can offer you wise counsel, who are willing to say what you need to hear instead of what you want to hear. That may start at home with parents and other family members. But don't rely just on your family. Seek out folks at your school, in your neighborhood, in your career field, and most important of all, at your church (if you don't have a church, find one!). I wouldn't be where I am today without Lou Holtz and Pastor Whitley. They are the kind of people who are motivated to invest their time and pass on their wisdom to others. If you look for them and are open to their teaching, you'll find those same kinds of people ready to invest in you.

7

EVEN HEISMAN WINNERS GET HUMBLED

A man wrapped up in himself makes a very small bundle.

BENJAMIN FRANKLIN

Sunday, September 4, 1988. Los Angeles Memorial Coliseum. Nearly forty thousand screaming fans in the seats, hundreds of thousands more watching on television. Blue skies and eighty-two degrees. It was a perfect afternoon for watching the San Diego Chargers take on the host L.A. Raiders in the season opener for both teams.

Except that I was too nervous to enjoy it. It was my first game in the National Football League.

The Los Angeles Raiders had chosen me in April with the sixth pick of the NFL draft. I'd been told I'd be a top choice, maybe even number one. But then the Atlanta Falcons, who held that first pick, announced they'd be drafting linebacker Aundray Bruce. My agent, Marvin Demoff, and I checked the rosters of the next few teams at the top of the draft. Most of them needed big-time help. We figured they'd be looking for a "savior," someone to step in and immediately lift the team to new heights. The exception to that scenario was the Raiders. That was where I wanted to go. To this day, I still don't know what Marvin said to those other teams, but they all passed me by.

You see, I didn't know for sure if I would make it as a wide receiver in the NFL. My last year at Notre Dame, running the wishbone offense, we'd emphasized the ground game more than passing. I did make thirty-nine catches for 846 yards, but I knew I still had work to do as a receiver. It was my punt and kickoff return ability that had made the difference in me becoming the first wide receiver to win the Heisman and in getting the attention of NFL teams. The Raiders, who already had a talented group of receivers, seemed like the right fit.

I did have confidence that I could succeed in the league as a returner. That assurance seemed to melt in the afternoon sunshine, however, when I stepped onto the Coliseum grass in the second quarter of that opening game. The Chargers had kicked a field goal to pull within 7–3. Now it looked like I was going to touch the ball for the first time as a pro.

Did I mention I was nervous? You could call that an understatement.

Before I knew it, the ball was high in that perfect sky. I gulped, remembered that we had a left-side return on, and moved to make the catch on the three yard line. I ran to the middle to try to draw everybody in. When I reached the twenty, I veered left, where my blockers were set up.

Later, when I saw the video, I realized just how nervous I must have been. While running to the left, I had the ball in the wrong hand, my right, instead of protecting it from would-be tacklers in my left. I never do that, but on this play, I did. Fortunately, it didn't matter.

My blockers did their job beautifully. I saw an opening and turned on the jets. By the time I reached the thirty, I was running past everybody—it was over. At that point, I was so scared and running so fast, no one could catch me. At the Charger ten yard line, I almost stopped running so I could turn, look at everybody, and say, "Is this really happening?" It felt like a dream.

I thought, *Hey, you can do this in the NFL. It's just like what you've been doing in junior high, high school, and college.*

That return definitely boosted my confidence, but playing in the pros was still in many ways a different world. The players were all bigger, faster, and stronger—not to mention meaner and uglier. Some were a lot older too. How was a guy who'd just turned twenty-two supposed to relate to teammates who were thirty-five?

Some of these guys were established stars and future Hall of Famers, including James Lofton, Howie Long, and Mike Haynes. None was a brighter star than Marcus Allen, the running back from USC who'd been named to five Pro Bowls and had won league and Super Bowl MVP awards. To a rookie, these players were pretty intimidating.

Fortunately for me, Marcus himself went out of his way to make me feel comfortable. He had a commanding presence—he's a lanky guy with long arms, so he looked bigger than his six feet two inches. And his ability to lead a team was off the charts. Nobody worked harder or played smarter. Yet he was constantly in my ear, telling me, "This is what's going to happen" or "This is how you're going to feel." It was amazing to be encouraged by a great player who wanted me to do well.

We had another personality on that team who was in a class by himself: Bo Jackson. Like Marcus and me, Bo was a Heisman winner from Auburn. Nike's famous "Bo Knows" advertising campaign had yet to infiltrate popular culture, but Bo was already a star. His talents extended beyond football, as he also played major league baseball for the Kansas City Royals. Because of his commitment to the Royals, Bo didn't join the Raiders until halfway through the season. He was so talented that it was worth it for the team to have him part-time.

You couldn't help liking Bo. He was confident but humble, with a fragile psyche and a serious stuttering problem. His first game during my rookie year was against the New Orleans Saints. In the first thirty seconds, he broke out on two long runs totaling forty-five yards. I'll never forget what happened next. Bo jogged off the field while unstrapping his helmet. A coach implored him to get back out there.

"No, Bo done for day," he said.

Incredulous, the coach told him to get a quick drink of water and get back into the huddle.

"Bo's hamstring tight. Bo done."

One more attempt by the coaches to get Bo back in the game was met by, "No, Bo done for day."

A few minutes later I looked over at Bo. He was sitting on his helmet eating a bag of peanuts. He knew he couldn't continue and just stopped. Bo done for day.

Adjusting to my new teammates proved easier than adjusting to the NFL lifestyle, or at least the Raiders' version of it. The plane rides to and from away games were always interesting. I preferred to sit up front, away from the card games and gambling going on in back. Some guys lost as much as fifteen or twenty thousand on the way to a game. I didn't understand how a player could have a good mind-set for a game right after throwing away all that money.

Some of the guys also brought huge bottles and jugs of alcohol on board. Win or lose, they were ready to let loose after the game. Many had to be driven home after we landed back in L.A. The Raiders were known as a blue-collar franchise, a hardworking, hard-living, hard-partying team. I respected the blue-collar, hardworking part, but the partying wasn't for me.

I also had to get used to all the free time and the length of the season. On Mondays, we were done with practice at noon. We had Tuesdays off. Saturday, we were done at ten-thirty in the morning. At first, it seemed weird not having to go to class and not having most of the day structured. Then it was great. But by November, I was dragging. I was used to an eleven-game season at Notre Dame, twelve if we made a bowl game. In the NFL, you had twenty games counting the preseason, then playoffs on top of that.

Near the end of the season, I felt so tired on some days that after practice, I went home to my townhouse in Manhattan Beach, ate dinner, and was in bed at six-thirty or seven. I was worn out.

———

Despite the adjustments, my first year in the NFL was incredible. The Raiders had outstanding receivers: James Lofton, the veteran; Willie Gault, the speed guy; Mervyn Fernandez, the dependable fifteen-to-twenty-yard receiver and my roommate; and Jessie Hester, the specialty route runner. These guys were established pros and I was a rookie, and they made sure I knew it. In training camp, I had to carry their helmets and shoulder pads, and pay for everybody's dinner any-time we went out together.

Even so, it was a great group. Willie had been brought in to replace James, the aging star, which had to have been difficult for someone who'd been a premier receiver for so long. For the first time in years, he was competing for playing time. Yet James in particular took the time to work with me and show me how to improve my game. I've always appreciated that. Because of the quality and experience of those four, I didn't expect to play much that first season. I was happy to contribute by returning kicks and working to improve as a receiver.

Midway through the season, I tore cartilage in my right knee. For a while it looked like we might opt for surgery and my year would be done. But after a couple of games with limited playing time, my knee felt pretty good, and I believed I could play regularly again. Then Mervyn got hurt. And then Willie. And then Jessie.

Suddenly James and I were the best options the Raiders had at receiver. I needed to step up.

A 17–10 victory over the Kansas City Chiefs was my first big game at receiver. I caught eight balls for ninety-five yards, including one for thirty-one yards. Later, in a 35–27 loss to the Seattle Seahawks, I made four catches for 114 yards and a touchdown, including a forty-nine yarder. I was just trying to make the most of my opportunity to play.

To my surprise, I finished the season as the team's leading receiver. What didn't surprise me was that my strength was still as a punt and kickoff returner. I led the league with 1,098 kickoff return yards and a 26.8-yard average. I also topped the league in all-purpose yards with 2,317, which broke Gale Sayers's rookie record and still stands today. My strong NFL start didn't go unnoticed either—despite my rookie status, I was named to the Pro Bowl as a kick returner.

As a team, our season was disappointing. The Raiders finished with a 7-9 record, leaving us in third place in the West Division of the American Football Conference. I was definitely excited about my individual performance, however, and I believed good things were ahead for the Raiders. Now, with only a few days remaining before Christmas, it was time to go home.

My return to my parents' home in Dallas was an event. I hadn't been there since early in the summer, before training camp. My younger sister, Kathy, was the only Brown child still living with Mama and Dad, yet all my sisters and my brother, along with nieces and other family, were gathering. That's just how the Brown family does it. If a couple of us are getting together, everybody gets together.

I have to admit, I was feeling pretty good about myself right then. Winning a Heisman Trophy, getting drafted in the first round of the NFL draft, and being selected for the Pro Bowl will do that to you. On the football field, it had been a mighty good couple of years. I'd never been a big talker about my achievements or gotten too full of myself, but no doubt about it, I was puffing up a bit.

Wayne picked me up at the Dallas airport and drove me home. When we pulled up at my parents' house, the first thing I saw was a paper banner strung across the porch, five feet long and three feet tall. It read: WELCOME HOME HEISMAN TROPHY WINNER/ PRO BOWLER TIM BROWN! Anyone in the neighborhood would have noticed it.

As I walked up the sidewalk, my chest stuck out a little. *Yeah, that's me*, I thought. *I'm the man.*

Mama was right there on the porch to greet me with a huge hug. "Timmy, I am so proud of you," she said.

"Thanks, Mom," I said. "I appreciate it. Love you."

After another hug, she glanced at the banner. "You see the sign we put up?" she asked.

"Yeah," I said. "It's nice."

"Do you know why it's out here?"

"No, I don't, Mama," I said. Little did I know that she was setting me up. "Why's it out here?"

To emphasize her point, she pronounced each word a little slower and a little louder. "Because all this," she said, waving her arm, "is going to stay outside. When you come inside, you're not going to be that person. You're going to be Timmy."

I'd been reeled in, hook, line, and sinker. In an instant, I went from "the man" with a puffed-out chest to a guy with his head down, muttering, "Yes, ma'am."

What I soon realized, however, was that my mom was doing me a huge favor. She stopped me from getting a big head before I could even get started. She hadn't raised me to act like I was somebody special and she was letting me know that nothing was going to change now.

It was actually a relief to hear that Mama didn't expect me to be somebody I wasn't. I'd started feeling that I had to be "Tim Brown, the Heisman/Pro Bowler guy," someone who had to impress and entertain everybody and do what celebrities were expected to do. But that wasn't me. It was refreshing to think I didn't have to turn into someone new.

My mom has never gotten caught up in my athletic accomplishments. She didn't even want me to play football because she was afraid I'd get hurt. My freshman year of high school, the only reason I was at our football games on Friday nights was because I played bass drum in the marching band. My sophomore year, I got my dad to sign the paper giving me permission to play football. Mama thought I was going to the games to play in the band. She didn't know I was on the team until she saw the "Sophomore Sensations" article in the paper. She wasn't too happy to learn that I was playing and that I'd gone behind her back.

Even after I started getting college football scholarship offers, Mama wasn't thrilled about my athletic efforts. I think she knew that sports sometimes has a way of warping a person's perspective.

Crazy as it sounds, she never did come to any of my high school or college games. She stayed home to pray for me instead.

All the attention and bright lights that come with being a star player, or being related to one, never interested my mom. She has always been a humble person. You knew it from the way she talked, the way she dressed, and the way she lived. My mother was all about being in church and serving and bringing glory to God. When that's your top priority, you don't have much need to heap glory on yourself.

I've been described as a gentleman for the way I carried myself as a player. I don't know how accurate it is to call anyone a gentleman in a game as violent as pro football, but I've tried to be a humble person, on the field and off. It has never made sense to me to showboat or try to embarrass another player. That first season, James Lofton told me, "Why would you want to do something that's going to upset somebody watching the film? Just hand the ball back to the official. You win the Super Bowl, you do whatever you want to do. But if you're not doing that, why antagonize people?"

So many of today's players, especially the younger ones, want to draw attention to themselves. They dance. They point. They scream in people's faces. That doesn't help them or their team. It just motivates the other side to work even harder to beat them.

The problem in many cases is the relationship these players have with their families. Most players' biggest fans are their relatives—and I don't mean that in a good way. The definition of a fan is someone who's fanatical, bordering on delusional. That kind of person will never see wrong in anything the player/family member does. If someone is always shown special treatment while growing up because of his athletic ability and is never told that the way he's behaving is low class and detrimental to the team, then by the time he gets to the NFL, he's not going to listen to reason.

These talented guys are continually booted off of teams that tire of their act. The second and third chances disappear in a hurry when they get hurt or just a little older and lose a step. Nobody wants to deal with their baggage. It's a rude awakening for them, and an all-too-common story.

A man needs a wife, a parent, a sibling, a friend, or a mentor who will tell him the truth about what they see. Someone who will gently but firmly point it out when he's disrespectful or too full of himself. Someone who will let him know that what he thinks is cool looks more like fool.

Of course, the need for truth-tellers and a humble approach isn't limited to football or even sports. People in all walks of life go about their day with a "Look at me, aren't I great?" attitude. Humility is just as important at the office, in the classroom, and at home. When we start thinking we're too valuable to do that menial project at work, we lose value in the eyes of the boss. When we begin believing we deserve that sports car, we blow our budget. When we feel we're above taking out the trash, we damage our relationship with our spouse or kids.

Putting too much stock in our own accomplishments and abilities and status detracts from the power and influence of God in our lives. Jesus said, "Whoever exalts himself will be humbled, and whoever humbles himself will be exalted" (Matt. 23:12). I've seen it in the lives of others and in my own life, and I have no doubt it will be even more obvious on the day I end up in heaven.

When I look back on my life and all the opportunities I've been blessed with, I have no doubt that the lessons my mom taught me about humility are a huge part of that. It's something I try to remember every day. I also know that if I forget, I can count on Mama to remind me.

8

A MAN TAKES RESPONSIBILITY

*A man must be big enough to admit his mistakes, smart enough
to profit from them, and strong enough to correct them.*

JOHN C. MAXWELL

In 1988, at the end of my first season with the Raiders, everything about my life in football seemed to be falling into place. That was definitely not the case, however, with my personal life.

I've already mentioned that starting in high school, I discovered something most guys figure out sooner or later—I really liked girls. Christy was my first girlfriend and I was smitten. She was everything I thought a girl should be. But she was also, as they said in the day, "fast"—faster than me by a long shot. After we'd been together for many weeks, my friends began giving me a hard time for not going all the way with her. They teased me in the hallways at Woodrow and called me a punk in front of other girls.

I knew the score from my Sunday school lessons—premarital sex was a sin. If you wanted to truly walk with God, you did not engage in sex before marriage. The long-term consequences, both to your health and to your relationship with Him, were not worth the short-term fun. My mind understood this, but my body seemed to have other ideas. I resisted for as long as I felt I could, but whether it was teenage hormones, peer pressure, or the fact that I believed I was in love, I gave in. Christy lived with her aunt, who often wasn't around when I visited their house during the evening. After I turned sixteen, Christy and I had sex, and lots of it.

If you're a young man reading this, I want to say right here that you shouldn't and don't need to take the path I took. There's a simple solution to the problem, which is to stay out of tempting situations. Tell your girlfriend where you stand on the issue, then figure out a strategy for avoiding potential trouble—that is, being home alone—and stick to it. The Bible says, "But run away from the evil desires of youth" (2 Tim. 2:22 NCV). That doesn't mean hang out for as long as you think you can and plan to walk away when things get too hot. It means run, right now! It's not easy, but you can do it.

At the time, I didn't feel guilty about what Christy and I were doing—that was one of the consequences that would come later. But I knew it was wrong. I realized my mom would be disappointed if she knew (while my dad probably would have given me a high five). But the worst part was understanding that God was displeased with my actions. I didn't see it at the time, but the longer it went on, the harder it was for me to be close to God. It drove a wedge between us that halted my spiritual progress for far too long.

Christy and I stayed together all through high school. I was still devoted to her when I entered Notre Dame. How devoted? I was the guy walking around campus wearing a T-shirt with our picture on it. At the end of my freshman year, however, I came home to devastating news. Christy confided that she'd been unfaithful.

I was brokenhearted and distraught. How could she? I'd been working hard at school and staying committed to Christy, and this is what I got in return? Christy's revelation that summer changed me. The anger that still simmered against my dad roared into a fire. I was mad at him, at Christy, even at God. When I returned to campus in the fall, I did little to pursue a relationship with Him. I rarely attended church services and never went to the famed Notre Dame Grotto to light a candle or pray.

I did, however, pursue relationships with other women. The better I played on the football field, the more opportunities I seemed to find around campus. Christy and I continued to date when I was home and I still saw us as a couple, but I was no longer the committed boyfriend I used to be. I remained too angry to worry if what I was doing was right or wrong.

That's how things stayed all the way up to the Heisman ceremony in December of my senior year. Back then, unlike now, the trophy winner returned to New York a few days after the announcement for a formal introduction into the fraternity. So on that second trip, Christy joined us.

With the Heisman Trophy in hand, graduation around the corner, and a pro career looming, this was one of the happiest times of my life. It was, at least, until that evening in New York. In my room at the athletic club, Christy and I got into a massive argument about my commitment to football and to her. We had very different ideas on what our future together would look like. By the end of that night, I think it was clear to both of us that our relationship was ending.

After seven years, it was tough to break up with Christy. But it left me free to spend as much time as I wanted with other girls during my last months on campus. That included romancing a beautiful sophomore I'll call "Ally." We quickly grew close. I was crazy about her.

On a May afternoon just before my graduation ceremony, I drove Ally to a South Bend bus stop so she could go back to her New Jersey home for the summer. Just before she got on the bus, she handed me a note. "Don't read it now," she said. "Wait until you get back to your room."

I kissed Ally good-bye, watched the bus drive off, and sat in my car in the bus stop parking lot. I was too curious about the note to wait. I unfolded the paper.

Ally was pregnant.

Oh, man.

I don't know how I managed to drive back to campus that afternoon. I couldn't see or think straight. When I got to my room, I sat on the sofa and cried. I was disappointed that we hadn't been more careful. I was disappointed that I'd put myself in this position in the first place by having premarital sex. I was sure God was pretty disappointed in me too.

I was twenty-one years old and definitely not ready to be a father.

I didn't tell anyone at Notre Dame about it. After I got home, I didn't tell anyone except my sister Gwen, and I swore her to secrecy. Over the phone, Ally and I talked about our options: keeping the baby, adoption, even abortion. I knew God wanted the baby to be born, but the final decision was Ally's. Later that summer, we met in St. Louis, where Ally told me she'd decided to keep the baby.

I could barely wrap my mind around it. Ally was going to have a baby—*our* baby.

Right after my first season with the Raiders, I told my mom what was happening. In her gracious way, she let me know that she was disappointed in me. The worst of it, she said, was that I probably wouldn't be around enough to be the father my child would need. That hurt, but she was right.

A few weeks later, on January 22, 1989, I was in Miami to watch the Super Bowl. I was about to leave the hotel for Joe Robbie Stadium when I received a page to call Ally. I found a phone and learned that we had a healthy new son: Taylor Donell Brown.

Wow. The news put a smile on my face. It also made my knees buckle for a moment. My world was about to change in a big way.

———

Several days later, after I'd played in the Pro Bowl, I was able to fly to Newark and see Taylor and Ally. I'll never forget that moment of holding Taylor in my arms and looking into his eyes for the first time. He was a beautiful little guy. It was mind blowing. Suddenly, it was all real.

As I held my new baby, my mother's words came back to me and I started to tear up. I knew I could stay for only a couple of days. Here I was, responsible for beginning this new life, and I wasn't going to be around to raise or even influence him. Even though I'd had difficulties with my dad, he had always been there. If he hadn't been around, I easily could have been pulled onto a destructive path. Who was going to prevent Taylor from doing that?

Back in Dallas a couple of months later, I heard a news report saying that because of the violence there, Newark was the worst city in America to raise an African-American boy. This wasn't where I wanted my son to grow up.

That report gave me an idea. Why should Ally and Taylor have to stay in New Jersey? Why couldn't they live in Dallas where I could keep Taylor during the offseason? I knew my family would welcome them with open arms. It might be hard for Ally's family, but I thought it was the best thing for Taylor. I called Ally and it wasn't long before she agreed with me. It would be another year before we made it happen, but I'm so glad we did.

Just before training camp in 1989, I returned to Newark so I could bring Taylor home to Dallas for a few days. We got him bundled in a car seat and I headed for the airport. At the terminal and on the flight, it seemed a hundred people stopped me to ask, "Where's the mom?" Every time I said she was home in New Jersey, their eyes widened and they said, "You have this baby by yourself?"

It wasn't a big deal to me. I'd always been good with kids. When I was younger, I used to babysit, change diapers, test the milk, do whatever needed to be done. I'd always hoped to have lots of children after I settled down and got married. The first time Mama heard that I might be a first-round NFL draft pick and come into some real money, she said with a groan, "Oh, Lord."

"What's the matter, Mama?" one of my sisters asked.

My mother responded, "Timmy's always said he'd have as many kids as he could afford!" She must have pictured me with about twenty little babies running around. That would have been a bit much even for me, but everyone knew I loved kids.

In May 1990, when Taylor was sixteen months old, we finally made the big move. Ally and I had picked out a place for her to live. I still lived with Mama, Dad, and Kathy during the offseason, so Taylor moved in with us until it was time for me to go to training camp. That became the routine for the rest of Taylor's childhood. He lived with me for half the year and with his mom for the other half. We both tried to give him as normal a childhood as was possible. It was the best solution for an imperfect situation.

Ally and I even tried to give our relationship another chance, but it just didn't work. We didn't connect in the way I'd hoped, and she had no interest in church. (Today, I'm happy to say, she's a strong believer and fully involved in her church.) But we helped each other as much as we could. She didn't go to the media about the pregnancy or put pressure on me to be there during the football season. I provided for her and Taylor financially and also made it very clear to my family and friends that Ally hadn't tried to "trap" me with a baby to extort money. She was a smart girl who'd given up a full academic scholarship at Notre Dame to have and raise Taylor, and she was someone I cared about.

I never thought about bailing on Ally and Taylor. I know it happens all the time in this country. A guy fathers a child out of wedlock and disappears soon after. But I couldn't imagine missing out on being Taylor's dad. More than that, I knew it wouldn't be right. I'd created this situation. I had to step up and take responsibility for it.

It was great having Taylor every year from January into July, and I missed him terribly when the season started. We were able to arrange a visit once or twice a season, but it was pretty tough to watch other players with their kids in the locker room and feel that Taylor should be there too, hanging out with me.

We established a regular phone routine during football seasons. I called Taylor every Sunday, Monday, Tuesday, Wednesday, and Thursday night. We often traveled on Fridays, and Saturday was my game preparation day, so I didn't schedule calls then. But on the other nights, we'd talk for ten seconds, ten minutes, or two hours, depending on what was on his mind. If I couldn't be with Taylor physically, I at least wanted to stay connected with him. I knew how important it was to be a regular presence in his life.

I'm so proud of Taylor today. As I write this he lives with us in Dallas, where he's studying nursing at Baylor University. He is incredibly smart (he gets that from his mother) and has grown up to be an amazing young man. Most of the credit for that goes to him, but I'd like to think that some of the choices his mother and I made also had something to do with it.

———

Take responsibility for your actions. That seems to be a problem for too many boys and men today. They make a mistake, whether it's spilling the milk or cheating on their wife, and their response is out of whack. They make up excuses. They blame someone else. They lie about it. They pretend it didn't happen. What they should be doing, however, is admitting that they screwed up and working double time to clean up their mess.

It's been an issue for us humans from the beginning. In the garden, after Adam and Eve both took a bite from the forbidden apple, Adam tried to blame it on Eve and Eve tried to blame it on the serpent. God's been listening to our excuses for a long, long time.

It isn't made any easier for us when our role models let us down. A young boy watches his father accidentally scrape someone's fender in the parking lot and quickly drive away without leaving a note or trying to find the other car's owner. What life lesson do you think that boy takes away from his trip to the store with dad?

I've been fortunate. I can't imagine my parents or Pastor Whitley or Lou Holtz trying to cover up a mistake like that. They were there for me as I grew up and matured into a man, and they provided the example I needed. Of course, whether we have a good role model, a bad one, or none at all, the decision on how we respond to our mistakes is up to us.

I'm also fortunate in that I had the financial resources to take care of Ally and Taylor and move them to Dallas. I realize that many men wouldn't have that option. But I'm a firm believer that sons and daughters need their father whether they live with him or not. We need to find a way to physically be there as much as possible, whatever it takes.

I'm reminded of an incident at the end of my junior year at Notre Dame. Unlike most colleges at the time, Notre Dame's football players lived in the same dormitories as the rest of the students. Juniors got first choice of available rooms for their senior year, and under our lottery system I had second pick for my preferred dorm. Everyone wanted one of the two rooms with a private bathroom, including me. I was already looking forward to my leisurely morning showers.

Sign-up day arrived. I happily made my pick at the selection table and went back to my room. A few minutes later, one of my classmates showed up.

"Tim, what happened, man?" he said. "I thought you were going to take the room with the bathroom."

"I did."

"No you didn't. *I* got 408. You took 403."

I suddenly realized I must have got the numbers wrong. I couldn't believe it.

My classmate saw the look on my face. "Hey, it's no problem. I know you were going to take that room. Let's just go down to the rector, make the change, and move on."

That sounded good to me, so off we went. We were laughing as we approached the rector. I figured we'd straighten out this little problem in no time.

"Hey, I made a mistake and chose the wrong room for next year," I explained to the rector. "But we've agreed to switch."

The rector just looked at us, unsmiling. "No," he said.

"Um . . . what do you mean by 'no'?" I said.

"You've made a mistake," the rector said, "and now you're going to have to live with it." He even told us there would be consequences if we tried to change rooms without telling anyone.

Did that seem rigid and unfair at the time? Yes, it did. But did it teach me something? Absolutely. When you make a mistake, you have to deal with the fallout. That means confessing to what you've done, doing what you can to repair it, and accepting the result. It doesn't mean making excuses, getting angry, or pointing fingers at someone else. The problem isn't the person you're pointing at, but the person you see when you look in the mirror.

Part of the issue, for men, is pride. You don't like to admit that you're fallible, and neither do I. It feels weak to say you're wrong about something. But I can guarantee that you're going to be wrong many times in life and that you're going to make plenty of mistakes. You might as well decide now how you're going to handle it when it happens.

Hopefully, you have a voice inside your head that lets you know when you've messed up and need to 'fess up and take responsibility for what you've done. Many people call that voice their conscience. For me, that voice is God. No matter how bad I've blown it, I know that when I listen to Him, He'll show me how to make it better.

9

A MAN IS MENTALLY AND PHYSICALLY STRONG

Our bodies are our gardens—our wills are our gardeners.

WILLIAM SHAKESPEARE

My career in professional football nearly ended just after it started.

We opened the 1989 season, my second, by hosting the San Diego Chargers at the Los Angeles Coliseum. Partway through the third quarter, it had already been a busy day for me. I'd returned four punts and two kickoffs, and caught one pass for eight yards. When Marion Butts ran in a one-yard touchdown to bring the Chargers within two touchdowns of us at 28–14, it was time for me to get on the field for another kickoff.

I caught the ball and veered left. We were set up for a middle return, and it looked like this could be a big one. I was just past the twenty when a big number 59, San Diego's Ken Woodard, came my way. I tried to plant my left foot so I could cut back to the middle. It was a move I'd made a thousand times, one that should have had the defender grabbing for air. But on this day, the Coliseum grass didn't hold my cleats.

My left leg slid and extended. I was an easy target. Woodard hit me in the right shoulder and crushed me into the turf. As I struck the ground, I felt my left knee bend and something in my leg collapse. It didn't hurt (I found out later I'd torn nerves, which explained the lack of pain), but something felt loose. I stayed down.

The trainers came onto the field to check me out. One held up his hand. "Tim," he said, "how many fingers do you see?"

I shook my head. "I wish it was my head," I said. "It's my knee."

I walked off the field without help. In fact, I wanted to play more. We were having a great game and I wanted to be part of it. "C'mon H-Rod," I said to trainer Rod Martin as I sat on the sideline. "I want to get back in. Let me go back in."

"Timmy," he said. "Look at your knee."

I looked. It was like a gate swinging in the breeze. My kneecap was on the left side instead of in the middle. I knew this wasn't good.

It turned out I'd torn my medial collateral and posterior cruciate ligaments, two of the four major ligaments of the knee. The combination of the two was a rare and significant injury. I needed surgery at Cedars-Sinai Hospital the next morning. My season was over.

The news got even worse just before I was wheeled into the operating room. The doctors weren't sure if my knee would be all right after the surgery. They were talking more about trying to get me to walk straight than if I'd ever play football again. One doctor said, "It's probably time to start looking at other ways to make a living."

Those weren't the words I wanted to hear, but I wasn't shocked. I already knew the situation was serious. Actually, right after that conversation, I felt thankful. I kissed my Notre Dame class ring before handing it over to a nurse. My parents had always emphasized how important it was to get a college education, something they'd never had the opportunity to pursue. I'd earned a sociology degree with a minor in business. I knew that if this was the end of my football days, there were still other things I could do in life.

A couple of weeks later, I started rehab with the Raiders' trainers. My Monday-through-Friday workouts focused especially on leg lifts as we tried to build back strength in my knee and leg. The workouts ended with what the staff called "hell time." I had to lie on my stomach on a table while a trainer used his shoulder to bend my lower leg back toward my body. The idea was to go a little farther each day and eventually break up the scar tissue in my knee. If I heard a *pop*, I knew it was working. I also felt the worst pain I'd ever experienced. I wouldn't wish those knee cranks on anyone.

———

As the weeks passed, my progress seemed to falter. In November, fellow receiver Mervyn Fernandez pulled me aside. "Dude," he said, "they need to go back in and fix you up. They obviously didn't do it right."

That was a tough time. I wanted to be back on the field with my teammates, who were on their way to an 8-8 season. Now I was having issues with my rehab. I wondered what kind of NFL career I had left.

Finally, in December, the trainers and I went to a specialist. He gave them a bad time for the rehab program they'd been using on me and showed them ways to twist and massage my knee and leg. The new plan worked. Within a week, I was making progress again.

Six months after the injury, the staff told me the knee was healed, that we just needed to add range of motion. But they kept babying it, preventing me from doing anything close to what happens on a football field. Finally, I'd had enough. I had to know.

"We need to find out now if this thing is going to work next season or not," I said. "Let's see if everything's healed in there. Let's put it to the test."

I convinced the trainers, Rod Martin and Todd Sperber, to join me on the goal line on one of our practice fields. "I'm going to run, spin, cut, double juke, triple juke, everything I can do to see where we are with this knee," I said. "If I make it through, I hope everyone'll be satisfied and we can go full speed ahead. If I don't make it through, then we'll know we've got an issue and we have to go back in and get this thing redone." They weren't excited about it, but they were willing to let me try.

With a deep breath, I took off. I sprinted. I ran routes. I put moves on phantom defenders. After months of rehab and confinement, it was great to be out in the open, just cutting loose. Before I knew it I was at midfield, then the forty . . . the twenty . . . and the opposite goal line. Running those hundred yards into the end zone felt as good as any kickoff I'd ever returned for a score.

The trainers and I met near midfield, in front of the entrance to the locker room. "All right," I said, "is everybody satisfied now? Let's get to work."

———

As much as a football player depends on his body to thrive in the ultracompetitive NFL, the first step to success actually takes place in his mind. It's all about attitude. That's especially true in relation to injuries. Every player who takes the field risks the chance of a season-ending or career-ending injury. But it's critical that he put those thoughts out of his mind. The player who enters a game focused on not getting hurt is a liability to his teammates. He'll be tentative and likely out of position, which actually makes him more likely to end up injured.

That's one of the reasons I always wanted to get back in the game as fast as I could after I'd been hurt. I didn't want to allow myself even a moment to doubt my ability to perform or think about the possibility of injury.

In 1990, my first season after the knee surgery, we played it cautious in the first preseason game. Once I got through that obstacle, though, I went full out. I didn't have any problems, but it wasn't until our third game, a victory over the Steelers, that I truly believed I was back. I returned three punts, including one for more than thirty yards, and also caught a pass. More important, I just felt right. I could turn on my usual burst of speed when I needed it.

I went home excited that night. My NFL future looked bright again. When I woke up, however, I had a problem. I couldn't straighten or flex my knee.

Uh oh.

I limped into the Raiders facility later that day, walking on tiptoe with my left leg because I couldn't put it flat on the ground. "What are you doing?" Rod Martin asked me.

"Man, I can't walk."

"Don't be playing around," he said.

"No, I'm serious."

H-Rod's face turned white. "Well, we'll have to wait for the doctors. It's one of two things. Either you tore an adhesion, which is a good thing, or you ripped something. And that's a problem."

Soon a doctor arrived, who drained fluid from my knee. When

that syringe started filling up with a pinkish liquid, I thought it was blood. "No, no, no, that's not good," I said.

"No, Timmy, that's not blood," someone said. "You're all right." Once they finished draining my knee, I was good as new.

Injuries and the fear of getting them can drive a player crazy. You're healthy. You're hurt. You think you're rehabbed but you're not. You think you've reinjured yourself but you're okay. If you dwell on it, you get yanked up and down like a yo-yo.

That's why it is so important to be mentally strong. You can't play scared in the NFL. Yes, you need to be smart and protect yourself. If there's a fumble, you don't just carelessly throw your body into the pile of players and expose yourself to serious injury. You want to be able to walk away and help your team on the next play. But at the same time, you can't be afraid to go after the ball. That's your job.

The worst thing for a player is to watch film of a game and see himself back away from blocking an opponent or not go for a catch because he's afraid of getting hurt. Receivers can develop what we call "alligator arms"—when they don't fully extend their arms while reaching for a ball because they fear taking a big hit. Once opponents see you with alligator arms, you never live it down. That's when it's time to get out of the game.

At least 90 percent of the guys on every team in the NFL are fully dedicated to doing all they can for the team to win. But if three or four or five guys aren't selling out for the cause, they are the ones who often make the difference between winning and losing. Your attitude has to be, "I'm going to get it done no matter what."

The same is true for any aspect of life. The corporate manager worried more about losing money than about making deals that will take his company to the next level is a manager about to be replaced. The guy always afraid of saying or doing the wrong thing in front of his girlfriend isn't going to keep that girlfriend. A man has to approach his life with total commitment and confidence. That's an attitude of strength.

In my case, my injury did alter my thinking in one significant way. I believed my NFL career was likely to be short. I felt that every practice, every game, and even every play could be my last. I thought, *If this is my last one, I want to make it my best one.* Instead of holding back or worrying about getting hurt, I went the other way. I gave it my all on the field and my preparation for each practice and game, mentally and physically, was over the top.

How so? If we had a game scheduled for Sunday, I didn't talk to Taylor or my mother after Friday. I didn't have sex after Thursday. Yes, you read that right. I wanted to save all my energy for the game.

Saturday was my day to get in the zone. I went to morning practice and was home by eleven. Sometimes I watched the Notre Dame game on TV. Otherwise, I sat by myself. In my mind, I went through the upcoming game, the plays we planned to run and the likely response of the other team's players. My thoughts ran something like, *How am I going to deal with this guy? I might need some help on this play because I might not be able to handle the crackback block by the linebacker.* Some guys took the opposite approach. They wanted to stay active on Saturdays and put football completely out of their minds. But what worked for me was to be alone and focus.

On game days, I did everything I could to stay in the mental zone I'd created. I was a monk—I didn't talk much to my teammates. Instead, I listened to my gospel music with a towel over my head, then lay on the floor and thought more about our plays, my routes, and the film we'd watched of the other team. By the time the whistle blew for the opening kickoff, I was so prepared mentally that I felt I almost knew what was going to happen on the field.

Of course, I prepared physically as well. I worked out hard, in season and out. I got my rest. On game days, I always stretched in front of my locker for thirty minutes. I taped ankles, wrists, and my big toes, and just before I walked onto the field I taped each joint on my fingers. I often applied heat plasters to my back, hamstrings, and hip flexors. I added extra padding to my shoulder pads. If you watch film of me over the years, it looks like I was still growing—that's because I kept adding more padding as I got older!

You didn't see other guys on the Raiders preparing for games the way I did. When they got to the locker room, most of them were laughing, joking, and talking on their cell phones. It was only just before game time that they got serious. I'm not saying they were any less dedicated than I was, but the approach was different.

In the early years of my career, some of the veterans—guys like defensive end Greg Townsend and linebacker Jerry Robinson—used to give me a bad time over my routine. They'd lift up my towel, peek in at me, and chide, "Hey, you scared? Are you scared in there?" But once I made the Pro Bowl again in 1991, the teasing pretty much stopped. They saw that what I did worked for me.

I'll admit, my approach was a little OCD. But I thought it was necessary for me to be successful. And I never wanted to see my career end because I hadn't done everything I could to prepare myself mentally and physically. The two reinforced each other. By staying focused and mentally strong, it was easier to play well and stay committed to keeping my body in shape. And by knowing my body was at its best, it was easier to adopt a confident and strong attitude.

I believe that's true for any man. Even if he's not an athlete, he's going to perform better in his job and have better relationships when he feels strong in mind *and* body. He's better prepared to tackle that new project at work or help his wife or child deal with a challenge at home when he's at his best mentally and physically. My NFL days are over, but I still work out and often run with the high school track team I coach. I know what a difference that makes for me.

Staying strong mentally and physically is biblical, as verses like these show: "For God has not given us a spirit of fear, but of power and of love and of a sound mind" (2 Tim. 1:7 NKJV) and "Do you not know that your body is a temple of the Holy Spirit. . . . Therefore honor God with your body" (1 Cor. 6:19–20). It also just makes sense. When a man knows his mind and body are both in peak condition, he's ready to take on the world.

10

A MAN OVERCOMES TEMPTATION

Every moment of resistance to temptation is a victory.

FREDERICK W. FABER

In the first years of my NFL career, I was strong mentally and physically. It allowed me to perform at a high level in one of the most competitive and demanding professions around. But I had a weakness, an area where I wasn't strong. And the longer that went on, the more I struggled off the field.

I'm talking about my spiritual life.

As I've said, I put a barrier between God and myself when I started having sex in high school. It was something I knew He didn't want for me. That distance continued all through college. I made little effort to spend time with God and close our spiritual gap. The way I lived also contributed to the barrier. I wasn't a wild party guy.

I never drank or did drugs. But girls? That was another matter. I was definitely more focused on girls than God.

A small part of me knew I was in spiritual trouble before I joined the Raiders. When I visited Pastor Whitley just before my first preseason, he knew better than to pronounce his blessing on my self-absorbed plans. But I wasn't ready to hear his wisdom. Not yet.

When you take a guy who has just turned twenty-two and is crazy about girls, give him a lot of money for the first time in his life, make him something of a sports celebrity, surround him with new teammates and friends who are eager to introduce him to the NFL culture, and drop him into the middle of the L.A. party scene, you've got a recipe for trouble. It was a perfect storm of temptation, and when it came to girls I didn't put up much of a fight.

I didn't dive in right away, but by my third season with the Raiders, when I was twenty-four, I was indulging in some of the opportunities that came my way. I hung out with Magic Johnson and other celebrities on Friday nights. I also dated plenty of girls, including "Jocelyn," one of the Raiders cheerleaders. It got so crazy that a friend of Jocelyn's offered to hook me up with another beautiful friend of hers—but only if she could come over to my place after her friend left. As she put it, "You want to do breakfast, lunch, and dinner? Let's do breakfast, lunch, and dinner." I'm sorry to say it now, but at the time, juggling three girls at once sounded great to me.

The temptations were over the top, yet I had my limits. Whenever I was invited to the Playboy Mansion, I always said no. I'd heard about some of the things that went on there. Whenever I was on the plane ride home after a Raiders game and a flight attendant invited me to an orgy, I always told her, "Thank you, I appreciate it, but I'm going to pass on that." Yes, L.A. is a freaky place.

Part of the reason for holding back was that I still had Pastor

Whitley's words in my head, even though I wasn't consciously listening to them. The other part had to do with an incident at the end of my first season at Notre Dame. We'd been invited to the Aloha Bowl in Honolulu. As a brother who could swim, I was a bit of an anomaly. I'd grown up swimming in pools in Dallas and had just passed a college swim class, so I couldn't wait to check out the clear, aqua water off the beaches of Waikiki. Right after we checked into our hotel, I was on the sand grabbing a boogie board.

I ran into the water, climbed on my board, and started paddling. A few minutes later I heard a couple of my teammates yelling, "Tim! Tim, you're going out too far!" I laughed. These guys couldn't swim. They were afraid of the water. I kept paddling.

The sun on my back and water on my hands and arms felt great. I decided I could get used to this. Finally, though, it was time to stop paddling and see how far I'd come.

Oh, man.

My friends on the beach looked an inch tall. I was hundreds of yards away. How was I going to get all the way back? How was I going to fight through the rough waves? Were there sharks in these waters? Right there on my boogie board, I started crying. No way was I going to make it back alive.

By the grace of God, the currents and my strong arms were enough for me to paddle back to shore. When I was close enough, my friends ran into the water and dragged me onto the beach. "We told you not to go in that water," one said. "We told you!"

I was too exhausted to answer. I just lay on the sand, feeling thankful to be alive. That's when a voice whispered inside my head, *Just as you almost went too far in this water, you can go so far away spiritually that you'll never get back to God.*

Was my head trying to remind me of what Pastor Whitley had said? Was God Himself giving me a warning? I still don't know for sure. But the message stuck with me, and it helped protect me during those crazy days in Los Angeles.

I tried to rationalize the women and the sex. I told myself, "The girls here are so beautiful and so nice. Why would I want to give this up? It must be right because it's all happening so easily."

But deep down, I knew that just wasn't true. The Bible says, after all, "It is God's will that you should be sanctified: that you should avoid sexual immorality" (1 Thess. 4:3). I eventually confessed my conflicted feelings to one of the girls I dated. Her solution was that we read the Bible together after we made love. I knew that wasn't the answer.

I made the Pro Bowl in 1991, and again in 1993, which started a run of five consecutive Pro Bowl appearances. The Raiders won the division title in 1990 and also made the playoffs in 1991 and 1993. But I found it harder and harder to enjoy my football success. My smile was only a half smile. I wasn't being the man I wanted to be or the man God had called me to be.

It got so bad that I started cutting myself while shaving my face in the morning. Not on purpose, mind you, and nothing requiring hospitalization. Just a little nick here, a little blood there. It wasn't because the razor was too sharp or because I was in a hurry. It was because I shaved in the dark. I couldn't stand to look at myself in the mirror.

In fact, I often stood in the bathroom with the light off, down on myself, angry and full of self-doubt, hoping for a sign that it was time to change my life and stop giving in to temptation. Of course, the fact that I couldn't look at myself in the mirror should have been the only sign I needed.

I sometimes felt as if I were losing my mind. Something was wrong with my soul. They say that you have to hit bottom before you can start to climb back up. I might not have been on the bottom, but I was close enough to see what it looked like. It was a scary view.

Sexual temptation is a big problem in America, especially for men. Let's face it, we're visual creatures. We're wired to enjoy looking at beautiful women. There's a reason why movies and TV and magazines and billboards and the Internet constantly bombard us with enticing female images. The directors, editors, and advertisers behind the media assault know how to get our attention.

Guys are tempted sexually not just every day, but every hour and seemingly every minute. That is part of the reason why premarital sex, affairs, divorce, and pornography are so prevalent today. And the temptation isn't just from the media. It's often the girls themselves, either in the way they dress or the way they walk and talk. As I discovered in L.A., it can be as direct, free, and easy as an offer for "breakfast, lunch, and dinner."

None of that is an excuse for giving in to temptation. But it sure makes it harder.

For me, once again, the answer to the problem is God. The Bible says that "No temptation has seized you except what is common to man. And God is faithful; he will not let you be tempted beyond what you can bear. But when you are tempted, he will also provide a way out so that you can stand up under it" (1 Cor. 10:13).

That verse both makes a lot of sense and gives me a lot of hope. Is sexual temptation "common to man"? In this world, absolutely! Yet God promises that it won't be too much for us—that He will also offer an escape. The catch is that you need to be walking with Him in truth and light to see it. When you're shaving in the dark, it's tough to see anything, let alone a way out of temptation.

Despite my clearly wayward lifestyle, God tried to get through to me. I remember accepting an invitation to teach at a football camp for young kids hosted by a member of the Seattle Seahawks. The campsite was in a remote field somewhere in Arkansas. On the day of the camp, I piled into a car with Philadelphia Eagle Jerome Brown and other players for the two-and-a-half-hour trip from the hotel to the site. It was the ride of a lifetime.

Jerome drove, which was a terrible mistake. He obviously had no fear of dying. He sped into oncoming traffic, crossed the median multiple times, and accelerated to triple-digit speeds. I held on to my seat so tight that my hands hurt and I privately prayed for God to save me. Another player, meanwhile, threatened to beat up Jerome if he didn't slow down.

Somehow we arrived safely. I was mortified to discover, however, that the "camp" was really a day-long party. After just an hour with the kids, the NFL players adjourned to a large tented area. Inside, alcohol flowed like rain, the scent of marijuana was in the wind, and men and women moved in and out of private tents.

This wasn't what I'd signed up for.

For the next hour I walked in a circle, my head down, talking to myself and God. I felt the pressure to be one of the boys and join in the fun, but I wanted no part of it. Then another NFL player, someone I didn't know, approached me.

"Tim," he said, "I've been watching you. I'll drive you back to the hotel if you want. This isn't the place for you."

Talk about a relief. I hadn't said a word to anyone, yet this stranger understood that I was freaked out. I believe God told that man to help me. He drove me back to the hotel before returning to the "camp."

If I'd been closer to God at the time, I think I would have seen that this day wasn't an exception, that He always provided an escape from the temptations around me. But I missed the lesson.

About a year later, I had another opportunity to heed a warning, this time about the consequences of our actions. While speeding in his hometown of Brooksville, Florida, Jerome Brown crashed his Corvette. Both he and his twelve-year-old nephew were killed.

I missed that lesson too. I didn't understand the significance of consequences. For Jerome, the consequences were his death and the death of his nephew. For me, it was the daily guilt and torment over the way I was living. The pain I caused other women when things got too serious and I had to cut them off. The memories I would bring into my marriage that couldn't be erased. The separation from God. If I'd known then what I know now, I would have chosen a different path. I would have trusted God more and looked for the "way out" of temptation that He promises.

If you're reading this and dealing with your own struggles over sexual temptation, here's my advice: take charge of your eyes and your thoughts. Slam the door shut before even a hint of temptation can sneak in. This also comes from the Bible. Do as Job did, who "made a covenant with my eyes not to look lustfully at a girl" (Job 31:1). Be like Paul and "take captive every thought to make it obedient to Christ" (2 Cor. 10:5).

How does that work? If a beautiful girl walks into your field of vision, you can't help but notice. You're a guy and you have eyes. But you *can* help what your eyes do next. This is the moment when you've got to look at anything else, even if it's the cracks in the sidewalk. It's simple—stop before you start. And if the girl begins talking and flirting with you? Again, don't hesitate. Let her know where you stand. If you're married, flash your wedding ring and start talking about your wife. If you're single, make it clear as soon as possible that you're interested in relationships that start with friendship, not sex.

Managing your mind can be a tougher proposition. When you

least expect them, sexual thoughts and images can scramble your brain. It doesn't help if you're regularly around an attractive coworker or a friend's beautiful wife. But the concept is the same. The moment your thoughts go astray, train your brain to focus on another, less dangerous topic. Maybe something like the Gross Domestic Product of Montana. Or better yet, the last Bible verse you read.

Sound impossible? Actually, it's not. Like the time I made a crucial catch in my first game at Notre Dame, a single victory with your eyes or mind over sexual temptation can give you the confidence to do it again the next time. Behaviorists say that it takes humans six weeks to form a habit. It's like a truck driving on the same dirt road. Keep going along the same sexually pure path for six weeks, and pretty soon you'll find the ruts so deep that it will be hard to drive out of them. That's the road to becoming a man.

My issue was sexual temptation. Yours might be something else: alcohol, drugs, gambling, pornography, even video games. Whatever it is, the same approach can succeed. Take control of your eyes and mind. Don't even crack the door to temptation. Look for the way out that God provides.

These principles work whether you're a man of faith or not. But when you have God in your life, you have extra ammunition for the battle. Sometimes the Holy Spirit—God in you—will even take charge and give you the words you need. That's what I believe happened one time on a flight home from Los Angeles.

It didn't take me long after I sat in my seat on the plane to notice a young flight attendant with a figure about as fine as it gets. I knew I'd better get my mind on something else, so I pulled out a newspaper and buried my head. But halfway through the flight, a pair of slender fingers appeared at the top of my newspaper and pulled it down. It was the same flight attendant, now sitting in the chair in front of me.

"You don't know who I am, but I know who you are," she said. "What are you doing once you leave here?"

The words that came out of my mouth were not what went through my mind. Tim Brown wasn't speaking. It had to be God.

"Hey, look," I said. "I met somebody six months ago. If not for meeting that person, there's no doubt in my mind what we'd be doing forty-five minutes after this plane lands."

"Oh, you have a girlfriend?" she said.

"I do have a girlfriend, and that's part of where I'm coming from," I said. "But the person I met is Jesus Christ."

That surprised her and ended any plans she had for us that night. But the devil was after me. He doesn't give up that easily.

About two weeks later, I joined my good friend and teammate Chester McGlockton at the Coliseum. He was hosting a program to get guns off the streets. People could exchange a gun for a game ticket. I was there to support the program and Chester.

The beautiful flight attendant was there, this time as a greeter on behalf of the Raiders. It turned she was also one of the team cheerleaders, a Raiderette. It wasn't long before she grabbed my arm. "Tim, c'mere for a second," she said. She pulled me into a corner with another attractive friend of hers.

"Look, we understand that you have a girlfriend and that you like God," she said. "All we're asking for is one night to party with you."

Suddenly it wasn't *I*. Now it was *we*. I was momentarily speechless.

But God didn't desert me. He sent a rescuer in the form of a six-foot-three-inch, 335-pound buddy. Chester spotted me in the corner and yelled, "Brown! What you doing there? Get over here, boy!" He rushed over and practically dragged me away from those girls.

They got the message and didn't bother me anymore. I got the message too. If I kept God at the forefront of my life, He would help me slam the door on temptation before it even had the chance to creep in.

For me, the answer to *every* problem and question has always been God. Many years went by without me understanding this truth. But in 1996, I was finally ready to figure it out.

11

FAITH IS FOR LIFE

Let us fix our eyes on Jesus, the author and perfector of our faith.

HEBREWS 12:2

God has been part of my life for as long as I can remember. One night when I was seven, I began to understand the spiritual forces at work in our world and how important my faith would be.

It was a Friday evening, and as usual I was in church with my family. Victory Chapel on Agnes Street was about as modest as it gets. The sanctuary wasn't much larger than a living room, so there was no falling asleep during the sermon. My uncle Johnnie was the pastor, and he could see you at all times.

This night was different than most services, however. My twenty-year-old cousin had fallen into a wayward lifestyle, and Uncle Johnnie decided it was time to give her some focused prayer. He called her up to the front of the church, then had us all gather round and lay our hands on her.

My uncle started praying. Suddenly, he pulled his hands away.

"There's demons in her!" he said. Uncle Johnnie told all of us kids to get our Bibles and put them over our chests to protect our hearts. Then he placed his hands on my cousin again.

She immediately backed away. In a low, guttural voice, she said, "I won't come out. I won't come out!"

Next, my cousin fell to the floor and started slithering and wiggling like a snake. Uncle Johnnie didn't hesitate. He reached down and grabbed her. "We have to get the demons out of you!" he shouted. "In the name of Jesus, I command you to come out now!"

My cousin started screaming, again in a low, masculine voice.

You'd better believe that I was freaked out. I'd never seen anything like it. There wasn't any green vomit like in the *Exorcist* movies, but the scene had everything else.

Twenty or thirty minutes later, it was over. My cousin had settled down, her expression changed from extreme agitation to a bewildered calm. The demons were gone. She didn't remember a thing about what had just happened.

I sure remembered, though. I could hardly believe what I'd seen with my own eyes. It was a lot for a seven-year-old to take in. I left church that night understanding for the first time that God was real, that there were both good and evil in the world, and that I'd better get on the good side with Him. It became an important step in my faith.

I took church and Bible studies more seriously after that night. As I've already related, however, my relationship with God sputtered for years starting in high school. The longer I pursued good times with women, the less I wanted to look in that mirror. I was a conflicted and unhappy man.

Early in 1996, I'd just finished my eighth year in the NFL and I was dating a beautiful recording artist. I loved "Vanessa" and we got along great, but somehow I knew that our time together had to end.

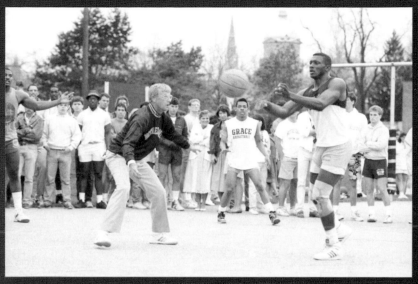

Bookstore basketball at Notre Dame. Coach Holtz was quite the competitor.

Seven Notre Dame Heisman Winners. Only picture we ever took together.

First game under Coach Holtz. First game as a wishbone back too!

Senior year at Notre Dame. More comfortable carrying the ball now!

Sharing the Commitment to Excellence Award with good friend Steve Wisniewski.

Rookie year, Pro Bowl.

My second Pro Bowl. Most satisfying after the knee injury my second year.

Me and Jerry getting ready at the 2003 Super Bowl.

Now Charles Woodson has joined in!

Second date with my future wife.

Couldn't wait for that boat to dock!

OPPOSITE PAGE: *(top)* Me, Cris Carter, Jerry Rice. At the time, the only three men to catch 1000 NFL passes. *(middle left)* One thousandth catch in Oakland vs. Jets, December 2, 2002. *(middle right)* NFL rookie year, Commitment to Excellence Award. *(bottom)* Celebrating with my daughter Timon after the 2002 AFC championship victory.

My spiritual inspiration: Mom.

Top row: Gwen, Joyce, Kathy, Ann.
Bottom row: Me, Pops, Mom, Wayne. Taken only a couple of months before we lost Pops.

My immediate family. Every Monday night the majority of us get together—yes, EVERY Monday.

My fam: Taylor, Ratisha, me, Sherice, Timon, and the twins, Tamar and Timothy Jr.

I realized that deep down I wasn't at peace with myself or with God. I'd been going about all my relationships in the wrong way. That sliver of evil I'd welcomed into my life—sexual sin—had created a growing, increasingly painful wound. I had to heal it. I needed to be in a relationship that honored God from the beginning, one where a woman and I could grow in our faith together.

Vanessa was ready to launch her career. I was finally ready to get right with God.

I received more confirmation of our diverging paths during a middle-of-the-night recording session early in the year. While Vanessa laid down tracks in a recording booth, I sat in the studio and tried to keep my eyes open. After several minutes, the producer asked his assistant to step out of the room.

When we were alone, the producer looked at me and said, "Tim, I've never met you. I haven't studied your history. I know only a little about you. But I could tell the minute you walked in that you're not comfortable here. I can tell you that it's not worth it."

I was confused. "What are you talking about?"

"This"—he gestured toward the studio around us—"is not where you want to be. This business is not for you."

The producer didn't know anything about the conversations Vanessa and I had been having about our future. I hadn't asked for a sign from God, but for that comment to come out of the blue left a big impression on me.

By June of that year, Vanessa and I were in the midst of a drawn-out breakup. I knew that she was in Chicago to tape an appearance on *The Oprah Winfrey Show* when I also got a call from one of Oprah's producers. I was immediately suspicious. I wanted no part of one of those "surprise" shows where the girlfriend suddenly walks on stage to talk with you about your relationship. If that's what they were selling, I wasn't buying. But the producer assured me that this show had nothing to do with Vanessa. They wanted to talk about community service.

I agreed to do the show and flew out to Chicago. The show went fine, but when I lost my wallet, I had a problem. I called Vanessa and she invited me to stay with her that night.

The two of us had a long talk. Vanessa didn't want our relationship to end. She wanted us to stay connected for life. She also wanted to start a family. In fact, she wanted to conceive a baby with me *that night.*

I was extremely tempted. I loved this girl. I also loved kids. The idea of having a reason to continue my relationship with Vanessa and of raising a child with her was definitely appealing.

But then I thought about Taylor growing up with a mom and dad in separate homes. I thought about how much I missed him when I was off playing football. Ally and I were doing our best under the circumstances, but it wasn't the proper way to raise a child. Now I was considering adding another kid to that equation? It wouldn't be fair to the child, to Taylor, or to Vanessa. It also wouldn't be what God wanted. What was I thinking?

"Vanessa, I love you," I said as gently as I could. "I love you so much that I'm not going to do this. Tomorrow morning or a week from now—or nine months from now—you'd regret it."

That might have been the toughest decision of my life to that point. But it was also the right one.

———

For the next two days, I mulled over the state of my life—particularly the spiritual side. I was almost thirty years old and ashamed of the way I'd been living. I had drifted away from the church foundation that my mom and many others had worked so hard to instill in me.

I'd separated myself from the powerful God I'd become aware of when I was seven. I had not heeded the words of Pastor Whitley to use my position as an NFL star to lead people to God.

I took an honest look at my faith and didn't like what I saw. I knew that God wasn't a heavenly genie I could turn to only when everything went bad. I also understood that as much as He loved me, He wasn't a buddy who winked at anything and everything I did. He was a powerful and loving God, yes, but He also demanded total commitment and obedience. I'd been a lot more committed to my football career than I had been to my faith. I'd been running from God for far too long.

I finally reached the end of my rebellion. On the night of June 26, 1996, I rolled out of bed at my parents' home in Dallas and got down on my knees.

I was ready to do business with God.

"Lord," I prayed, "I can't do this anymore. I don't *want* to do this anymore. I'm tired of trying to live a life I'm not comfortable with and that I know You're not comfortable with. It's time for me to stand up and be the man You want me to be. I need Your help— right now, tomorrow, and for the rest of my life."

I can't say that bells started ringing or that I heard the "Hallelujah Chorus." But I'd made my decision and it felt right. I was committing to be a spiritual man, not a "natural" man. I was giving my life to God. The challenge for me now, especially regarding women, was to live my life His way.

What I didn't realize was that God had been waiting for me. Now that I was finally on board with Him, He was ready to bless me with exactly what I needed.

The Lord's timing is always perfect. For a year and a half, my good friend and teammate Chester McGlockton had been trying to connect me with a girl from the L.A. apartment complex where he used to live. He had hired her to cook for parties he hosted. "Man, you need to meet this girl," he said the first time it came up. "She's a Christian, she's pretty, and she can cook. She's a nice girl."

You could say that Chester, in his day, had played the field too. "I know what your idea of a nice girl is," I said. "I don't want no part of your nice girls."

"No, Brown," he said. "I'm not talking about that kind of nice girl. I'm talking about a *nice* girl."

"Dude, I'm not falling for that one." I was sure Chester was trying to lead me into trouble. During rounds of golf or when we just talked, he kept bringing up the idea of hooking me up with this girl. I continued to resist what I viewed as an evil scheme.

It turned out that Chester and I were both moving in a new direction. He met Zina, the girl of his dreams and a Christian, in 1995. Chester began talking and behaving in an entirely different manner. We began having more and more conversations about God. He proposed to Zina, and then, early in 1996, he committed his life to the Lord.

That's how I found myself at a mansion in San Jose on July 6, 1996. Just ten days after I'd made my own commitment to God, I attended Chester and Zina's wedding. Before the outdoor ceremony, I sat down with a dozen or so NFL players. We were strategically positioned so that we could see everyone who walked into the courtyard. When an especially striking, dark-haired beauty in a polka dot dress arrived, everyone in our group sat up. Most started making comments, typically along the line of, "Oh, yeah, that's the one I'm going home with tonight."

I'd noticed this girl too, no doubt about it. But I was a new man. I had no intention of competing with these guys to try to take somebody home. I didn't even plan to talk to her.

It seemed that God had His own plan, however.

A few minutes later, I was waiting in line to get a drink and noticed the same girl right behind me. Competition or not, I figured I could at least be polite. I turned around and said, "Hey, what are you drinking?" She told me cranberry juice, so I got her drink for her. She thanked me, and we both moved on to talk to other people. End of story, I thought.

The wedding, held in the sunshine under a trestle, went off without a hitch. Chester's smile was big enough to light up Oakland's coliseum. Afterward, we gathered inside the mansion for the reception. Chester had designated seats for everyone. I found a place card with my name and sat down at that table. More people joined me until there was only one open seat, right next to me.

That's when the same girl showed up again. Chester had assigned her to my table too.

She and I made polite conversation during dinner. When they served carrot cake for dessert, I tried it—it was delicious. "Oh, man," I said to her. "You have got to taste this carrot cake." Without thinking about it, I cut a piece off with my fork and shoved it toward her lips.

The girl in the polka dot dress could have rejected this weird stranger who was trying to push cake down her throat. She could have embarrassed me and said, "Forget it, I'm not eating the germs off your cake." But she was gracious. She took the bite and said, "Oh, that *is* good."

That broke the ice. We started talking more, and kept on talking for the rest of the evening. Her name was Sherice Weaver. I was definitely intrigued. Unfortunately, I had to leave early to catch a flight back home to Dallas. When I got up to go, Sherice got up to head for the dance floor.

We had time for just a quick good-bye, but I wanted Sherice to know she'd gotten my attention. Earlier, I'd discovered that we had a mutual friend, Angie, so I asked Sherice if Angie could give me Sherice's number.

"No problem," she said with a smile.

On the way out, I interrupted Chester in the middle of a dance to say my good-byes. "Dude," I said, "who is this girl Sherice?"

"Man," he said, "that's the girl I've been trying to get you with for forever!"

Now it all fit. I knew more about this girl than I realized. I decided I wanted to find out even more.

I called Sherice the next day and left a message. The rest of Sunday came and went. Monday came and went. By Tuesday I was thinking, *This girl's not going to call me back.* She at least could've called and said, "It was nice meeting you but I'm not interested in dating right now." I wasn't even asking for a date. I just wanted to get to know her better.

Tuesday night, however, Sherice finally called back. We talked for six hours. Little did I know where those first conversations would lead.

That, at least, is how *I* remember the beginning of our relationship. Sherice has a different version—and I do mean different.

According to Sherice, believe it or not, I followed her around at the wedding from the moment I saw her. She says that I was behind her in the drink line, not the other way around, and *she* asked *me* what I wanted to drink. She says that as soon as I got my drink, I went over to Chester and said, "Who's that girl in the polka dot dress?" Chester said, "That's the girl I've been trying to introduce you to!" And I supposedly replied, "Oh, man! We'd be having a double wedding today if I'd just listened to you!"

That's not all. In Sherice's version of the story, Chester and I did some rearranging so that she ended up at my table. Then, according to Sherice, I tried to give her my number, but she wouldn't accept it.

So I gave my number to Angie and asked her to get Sherice to call me. Sherice wasn't sure she wanted to call, but over the next few days Angie persuaded her. When Sherice finally called on Tuesday, I supposedly said, "I thought I had bad breath or something—I didn't think you were ever going to call," which got us both laughing.

They say that love is blind. Maybe love has a bad memory too. I have to admit that Sherice is usually better at remembering those old details than I am. But somewhere in there is the true story, and as far as I'm concerned, the details aren't important. What counts is that God allowed me to meet the amazing woman I would be with for the rest of my life.

The timing of our first meeting couldn't have been better. I'd recently dedicated myself to God. Sherice, meanwhile, was just completing a six-month program based on a book by P. B. Wilson, *Knight in Shining Armor.* While "under construction," she hadn't dated men at all, focusing instead on her relationship with God and preparing herself for her lifelong love. It sure seemed like God had His fingerprints all over this thing. God used Chester to bring Sherice and me together. He also showed me that I needed to wait to meet her until we were both ready to begin a relationship that would honor Him.

God is like that. He wants to shower us with blessings if we'll only follow Him. It took me a long time to truly understand that and to start living a life of Christian obedience. As soon as I did, everything changed. I'm not saying that's always how it works. Sometimes He has work to do in us that takes years. Sometimes, even when we're fully committed to God, it can feel like He's forgotten us. Yet I have no doubt that the smart play, always, is to pursue His path.

Many a man, like me, has tried to go his own way and live a life inconsistent with God's teaching. As Jesus once said, you can't serve two masters. It doesn't work to live godly part of the time and do whatever you want or whatever feels good the rest of the time. My football career would have failed quickly if I'd taken that approach. The same is true for the Christian life.

Real success isn't based on money or fame or influence. It's about developing a relationship with God and letting all your thoughts and actions grow out of that. It's not a part-time gig, but a full-time, lifelong commitment. Is that often hard? No question about it. But the blessings God gives back—the joy, the peace of mind, the fulfillment that comes from serving and being close to Him—make it more than worth it.

12

A MAN ROMANCES A WOMAN'S HEART

A true man does not need to romance a different girl every night.
A true man romances the same girl for the rest of her life.

ANA ALAS

In the summer of 1996, I started my ninth preseason camp with the Raiders. We'd had some strong seasons, winning the AFC West Division in 1990 and making the playoffs in 1991 and 1993. We'd even advanced to the AFC title game in 1990, only to get trounced by Buffalo. I'd played for three head coaches—Mike Shanahan, Art Shell, and our current coach, Mike White—along with more quarterbacks than I could count.

I'd enjoyed personal success as well. In addition to making another Pro Bowl appearance, I was coming off a season with eighty-nine receptions for 1,342 yards, a 15.1-yard average. I also added 364 yards on punt returns. Now that Marcus Allen had moved on to Kansas City, I was one of the established stars and team leaders. At this point, we needed all the stars and leadership we could get. Al Davis had moved the team back to its original home in Oakland for the 1995 season, which was great for the longtime fans. Our record that year was just 8-8, though, and few expected us to improve on it in 1996.

I was as determined as ever to have a great season and to help my team win. Little had changed about my goals and life on the football field. Off the field, however, was another matter. My new commitment to my faith gave me a fresh perspective on everything. And I found my thoughts turning more and more to the girl in the polka dot dress.

After that first long call, Sherice and I continued to talk on the phone. All of those early calls seemed to go four or five hours. She was so easy to talk to and we seemed to have so much to say to each other. I wanted to learn everything about her.

I discovered pretty quickly that God was a high priority for Sherice, which definitely impressed me. Even as a child, she loved going to church and arranged to go with whoever would take her. Sherice dedicated her life to God at the age of eighteen, rededicated it after she turned twenty-three, and was baptized in 1995. Never much of a drinker, she gave up alcohol entirely and stopped going to clubs with friends. She began spending more and more time reading her Bible. She found that her desires were aligning with God's desires.

About a month after we met, I joined Sherice at a Los Angeles church for her Knight in Shining Armor graduation ceremony. The girls graduating at the church had read that by the time they completed the book and program, many would have already met their "knight." I didn't know about me being a knight, but Sherice was looking more and more like a princess to me. After the ceremony, we went out for dinner at a restaurant. It was our first date.

For our second date, I planned to take Sherice out to dinner again. But when I showed up at her apartment, I was completely taken by surprise. She'd set a fancy table and prepared an amazing candlelight dinner. I'm talking about Cornish game hens, wild rice, sweet and red potatoes, fresh green beans, brisket, and dinner rolls—the works.

"Who in your family is from the South?" I said. "Because West Coast folks don't cook like this." I'd had girls bake me cookies and give me Rice Krispy treats before, but no girl had ever made me a home-cooked, candlelight dinner. Everything was fantastic.

For me, that meal was the coup de grâce. Sherice embodied everything I was looking for in a woman and a wife. She was beautiful—which isn't the most important quality a man should look for, but in a romantic relationship you've got to be attracted to the girl. She was also utterly comfortable in social situations. I'd been with girls who stayed attached to my hip during social events because they were afraid to talk to people without me. With Sherice, if I had to check out of a conversation for a while, it was more like, "Oh, you go on, I'll be just fine," and she'd go right on talking as if nothing had happened. That was a quality I appreciated.

Of course, I'd heard from Chester that Sherice could cook, but I hadn't realized he meant she could *cook*. That dinner at her apartment blew me away.

More important than all of that, though, was the strength of Sherice's faith. She loved Jesus in a way that drew me to her. A friend had told her, "I've always noticed a certain light about you. When I'm around you, you make me want to be a better person." That's how I felt about Sherice. I could imagine a relationship with her that would also enhance our relationship together with God.

There was something exciting and freeing about starting a friendship with a woman that was based not on sex but on God and getting to know everything about each other. The truth is, I realized after those first three or four weeks of phone calls that Sherice was the girl I wanted to marry. I knew she was at least interested in me. Now I just had to show her how I felt and pray that if God wanted us together, He would allow it to happen.

Most guys are goal setters and problem solvers. If we see something we want or an issue that needs to be taken care of, we figure out how to fix it or get it, and we go for it. When it comes to romance, though, we can be a little clueless.

What I've learned is that women like to be noticed, appreciated, and pursued. They define romance as the things a guy does to make them feel loved, protected, and respected. Most important of all, they want to be heard and understood. They want a relationship that is heart to heart and soul to soul.

The great thing about the beginning of my relationship with Sherice was that because she lived in Los Angeles and I was based in either Dallas or the Bay Area, most of our first interactions were over the phone. We got to know each other in a deep way simply because we talked and shared so much. As my feelings for her increased, though, I knew I couldn't stop there.

I began sending cards and roses to Sherice every week. We each selected and shared a Bible verse with each other two or three times a week. When the season started, I sent a car to pick her up at work and take her to the airport so she could fly to my games. When I had a free Tuesday, I often flew in to have dinner and spend a few hours with her.

I also left voice messages for her at work. *Sports Illustrated* even picked up on that. Austin Murphy started an article about me by quoting one of my voice messages for Sherice: "Hello, my love. Just called to tell you that I missed you, that I thank the Lord every day for sending such a wonderful woman into my life." In the article, Murphy said I had "a romantic streak the width of Lincoln Kennedy,"[1] our 335-pound offensive tackle. I didn't see what I was doing as romantic, though. I was just expressing how I felt. I wanted to make Sherice smile every day. I wanted to let her know that someone viewed her as special.

My proposal definitely could have been more romantic. On a scale of one to ten, with ten being the top, mine was more like a 1.75. It was close to Christmas, and Sherice was coming up for our game in Oakland. I was too nervous to try something elaborate. I picked her up at the airport and took her to my place. After we got inside, I grabbed her and asked, "How much do you love me?"

"I love you a lot," she said.

I took a deep breath. "Do you love me enough to spend the rest of your life with me?" I pulled an engagement ring out of my pocket.

Sherice gulped. Then, thankfully, she said yes. We eventually set a wedding date of June 21.

Romance wasn't exactly on either of our minds during a conversation we had about three months into our engagement. Sherice joined me in Maui for an NFL Players Association meeting. Since the infidelity of a few star athletes had been making news headlines, Sherice and I sat down in my hotel room to have a frank conversation about athletes, the temptations of women, and marriage.

I now had my priorities in order. Nothing came before God in my life and I wanted to make sure Sherice knew it. She'd never have to worry about me cheating on her because God was higher on the list.

I looked Sherice squarely in the eyes and said, "I will always love God more than I love you."

That's probably not the most romantic thing to say to your fiancée. The words might have been a little blunt. From the expression on Sherice's face, I could tell she was hurt. I also told her that day that if she ever saw me doing something that would anger God, she should leave me because that meant I was probably doing ten other things she couldn't see.

I wasn't trying to sabotage my marriage before it started. I was just making it clear that my commitment to her was unquestionably founded on God. That, I believed, was crucial to the success of our relationship. Over the next few months, Sherice had the chance to fully digest my words and understand where I was coming from. Today, I still stand by my statement in Maui. And Sherice says she wouldn't want it any other way.

In some ways, it's still hard to believe that Sherice said yes all those years ago. It was a long journey for me to become the kind of guy a girl like Sherice would want to be with. I'm still working on it.

What did Sherice see in me? It had nothing to do with being a celebrity or football player. I still give her a hard time about that. She was a Lakers fan who paid almost no attention to the NFL. Her cousin was on the Raiders practice squad, so she had attended one of our games in 1995. She was in the coliseum the day I caught a twelve-yard pass from Jeff Hostetler, made a couple of moves, and turned it into an eighty-yard touchdown. I had five receptions that afternoon for 143 yards as we beat the Seahawks, 34–14.

Sherice says she missed all that. She claims she didn't even know who I was. "There's no way you didn't know who I was," I tell her, "so you can just stop with that."

"I wasn't paying attention to the game," she'll say. "I was talking to Melani, Rocket Ismail's wife."

"When somebody starts going eighty yards down the field," I say, "you stop talking and start asking, 'Who is that brother running like that?'"

It's an argument I never win. Either way, it's safe to say that

Sherice wasn't awed by my football success. What did get her attention, apparently, is that I didn't just talk about my faith. She saw me live it. In her words, "With Tim, what you see is what you get. He loved going to church, Wednesday, Friday, Sunday. He is who he is. He's real."

Another thing that impressed her was that I respected and shared her desire to practice abstinence. I'd learned my lesson there. I was looking at the entire woman, not just how fine her body was. It was a new experience for me—I was with one of the prettiest women I'd ever laid eyes on and I wasn't even thinking about sex. I'd discovered that when two people are physically intimate right away, it throws a roadblock into their relationship. It immediately takes things to a different level. Expectations change. It makes it extremely difficult to see that person for who she is. The ability to get to know her on a deep friendship basis goes out the window.

With Sherice, I developed a heart-to-heart, spiritual connection first. It was exciting in a whole new way. I couldn't wait to talk to her and see her. I almost wish we could have had a longer engagement so we could've gotten to know each other even better before our marriage. Don't get me wrong—as our wedding approached, I was definitely looking forward to the sex too. I wasn't planning on any five-year engagement! But the way our relationship grew was godly and special. The more time I spent with Sherice, the more I realized she was worth the wait.

You may be single or married, young or old. No matter where you are in life, there are a few things Sherice and I both believe you should aspire to, especially as they relate to your relationships with women. They start with sharing a strong faith in God. From my perspective, that's what everything else is based on.

You should also respect the values of your girlfriend or wife. If her boundaries regarding dating and your physical relationship are stricter than yours, they should become your boundaries too. And if hers are less strict and might lead either of you to stray from God's plan, you need to take the lead in setting limits.

Boundaries were especially important for Sherice because she was sexually molested when she was young. Even now, a touch on her shoulder in a certain way can bring back awful memories. For years, Sherice didn't talk about those experiences. I'm so proud of her for opening up about it more in the last few years. When she told her story to a group of women at a Super Bowl event, it was powerful. It gave many of those women the courage to say, "That happened to me too" and to start dealing with it.

The woman you're with may also have different values and ideas about parenting, finances, and all the other issues that come up in a relationship or marriage. You need to talk those things through. Don't just say, "Here's how it's going to be"—or worse, make important decisions without even letting her know. I've been guilty of that one with some business opportunities. When Sherice says with more than a hint of sarcasm, "Thanks for involving me in that," I know I've blown it.

Even if you're married and your wife agrees that the husband has the final say, make sure you see things from her perspective before you make a decision. When you really *listen* to her, understand what she's saying, and let her know you get where she's coming from, it makes all the difference as you go forward. That's what sustains your heart-to-heart connection.

Another way to keep that connection going is to find out what author and counselor Gary Chapman calls each other's "love language."[2] With Sherice, it's words of affirmation—she practically glows when someone notices she's done something well and says so. For me, it's physical touch. If you rub the back of my hand, I'm like a puppy wagging his tail. I'll soak that up all day. When you know what most speaks to a woman's heart, you can encourage her in ways that are especially meaningful.

Of course, when a man and woman get married, and especially once they have kids, it's easy to get so busy and locked into a routine that the romance starts to fade. Don't let that happen to you. There's a reason why so many marriage experts recommend regular date nights for couples—it's the real deal. As much as I love my kids, it's a beautiful thing when just Sherice and I can get away for time to relax, have fun, and renew our relationship.

When you put all of this together, you get what Sherice calls the complete Christian man. This is a guy who deeply loves God and his wife. He knows his wife's heart because he takes the time every day to listen to her and understand her.

Feel intimidated? You shouldn't. You *can* be that guy. Make God your foundation, be sure to regularly add a dash of romance, and you're practically there.

13

BE WHO YOU'RE MEANT TO BE

Men, like nails, lose their usefulness when they
lose direction and begin to bend.

WALTER SAVAGE LANDOR

I received what I thought was an important football lesson during my first year at Notre Dame. We were hosting Miami and had a 13–7 lead in the third quarter. Then Bernie Kosar started completing bombs for the Hurricanes and we couldn't stop them. Three touchdowns and a field goal later, they were up 31–13.

Near the end of the game, it was obvious we weren't going to pull this one out. A coach yelled, "Okay freshmen, get out there!" The coaches didn't want to risk an injury to our starters. It wasn't long before a pass came my way over the middle. When I jumped, I got blasted in the air by two guys—it felt like they hit me about eight times as they knocked the football from my hands and sent me to the ground.

Those two weren't satisfied with just making a big hit. They stood over me and started trash talking: "Eugene must be a real blankety-blank 'cause you're a real blankety-blank."

It freaked me out that they knew my dad's name and were using it to curse me. When I got to the sideline, I went to Mike Stock, our receivers coach, and said, "Coach, they're talking about my daddy out there."

I'll never forget what happened next. Coach Stock grabbed my jersey, got in my face, and said, "Son, this is big-time college football. If you don't change the way you play this game, you will not be around here long."

After the game, I went back to my dorm room and thought about what he said. "Okay," I told myself. "I get it." I figured my coach was letting me know I needed to be more like those Miami guys.

That was the beginning of my cursing on the football field. I used it to get myself pumped up, both at Notre Dame and even more so in the pros. I was pretty quiet my rookie year in the NFL and was out with my knee injury for my second year, but starting with my third season the nastiness flowed out of me like part of my breathing. I was already frustrated that season because of the coaches' plans to only use me on third downs and punts. Sometimes I started a fight with somebody right after I got in the game. It was so bad that my dad told my mom, "He may act like you off the field, but he acts like me when he's on it."

Then I had my reckoning with God. After that June night in 1996, I stopped the verbal outbursts against opponents. I figured I had this cursing stuff under control.

Turned out I was wrong.

For the Raiders, the 1996 season was worse than the year before.

We finished 7-9, tied for last in the AFC West Division and missing the playoffs for the third season in a row. Head coach Mike White was fired and replaced by Joe Bugel. We didn't start 1997 any better, losing three of our first five games. Our defense and running game were both ineffective, forcing us to rely heavily on quarterback Jeff George's passing.

I was playing well individually. In 1996, I recorded my fourth straight year with at least eighty catches and 1,100 receiving yards, and I started 1997 going at least 150 yards in three out of our first five games. But by the time we hosted San Diego on October 5, it looked like the Raiders were in for another long season. My frustration grew.

It didn't help my mood when San Diego kicked field goal after field goal and started to pull away from us. When Greg Davis connected on his sixth kick from thirty-three yards in the fourth quarter, the Chargers led 25–10.

It also didn't help that I couldn't even catch a cold in that game. I'm not talking about balls slipping through my fingertips but passes that hit me in the gut. I'd made just three catches for eighteen yards and had as many drops as receptions. It looked like I hadn't shown up to play that afternoon.

The game was nearly over when I lined up on the right side and ran a crossing route to the middle of the field. Once again, Jeff George's pass was on target, and once again, I dropped it. I took a couple more steps before strong safety Rodney Harrison leveled me with a hit to the shoulder. While I was on the ground, Rodney stood over me, laughed, and added a few insults in case I missed his meaning.

Rodney was a future All-Pro and very aggressive. I'm not saying he played dirty, but it's true that he didn't worry much about whether his hits came before or after the whistle. We had plenty of tough battles over the years.

After that hit at the end of the San Diego game, though, I didn't care if the opponent was Rodney Harrison or Daffy Duck. I'd had it with my lousy play, the losing, and the taunting. I stood, put my helmet next to Rodney's, and unleashed a profanity-laced tirade like never before, one I didn't even know was in me. I dropped so many forbidden words it would have made Chris Rock blush.

I finally realized how out of control I sounded, but by then the bell had been rung. I couldn't take it back. After the game, I attempted to apologize to Rodney, but he brushed it off. "Look, dude," he said, "what we do between the zeros is what we do."

I felt terrible on the drive home from the game, and not just because of my bad game and our loss. I was disappointed that in that moment I'd been such a poor example of a God-honoring man and that I'd probably lost any chance of ever influencing the faith of Rodney Harrison. I realized that even though I'd given my life to God I wasn't allowing His Spirit to help me day by day.

As usual, I had more than twenty family and friends coming over to my place after the game. But the first thing I did when I arrived at my condo was run upstairs to my bedroom, drop to my knees, and ask God to help me through every moment from that point forward.

I was excited about the idea of giving God control of my actions and my mouth on the football field, but it also scared me. How was I supposed to continue performing at a high level if I couldn't taunt and swear to get fired up? "Lord, this is how I play the game," I prayed. "This is who I am."

The answer wasn't audible, but it was a strong impression nevertheless. I sensed God clearly saying, *You don't have to play the game like that to be successful.*

It turned out—surprise!—that God was right. I stopped cursing and played better than ever. Although 1997 was an awful year for the Raiders, as we finished 4-12, it was statistically the best season of my career as a receiver. I caught 104 passes for 1,408 yards and averaged 88 receiving yards per game. Maybe relying on a foul mouth wasn't who I was after all.

That tirade against Rodney Harrison was the last time I cursed in my life.

Each of us is unique. God created us as individuals with a specific blend of gifts and characteristics that no one else can claim. We are, as the Bible says, "fearfully and wonderfully made" (Ps. 139:14).

With that in mind, it's important for us to figure out who we are—to understand what makes us both the same and different from everyone around us. I know, for example, that I can be outspoken and strong-willed. I also show my emotions easily. I am a creature of routine and in the right crowd I can be outgoing and carry the conversation.

I'm not what you'd call flamboyant. I don't have to be the guy everybody's always watching and talking about. So many athletes today seem to need attention. The over-the-top dress, the tattoos, the antics on the field, the trouble off the field—they seem to be shouting to the world, "Look at me!" It's as if they constantly need people to notice them and tell them how great they are because they don't believe it themselves.

I'm not saying I'm better than those guys. It's just that I'm comfortable with who I am. I don't need to hear how wonderful I am every day. I don't need to create an image or pretend to be something I'm not.

Image has a lot to do with the endorsement deals and other opportunities that often come an athlete's way. I have nothing against those deals. But I'm not going to change or play a stereotype to get one.

That has cost me in the past. I'd hoped to sign a big contract with a major apparel company once I started my NFL career. One company told me they'd sign me if I landed in a major market. When the Los Angeles Raiders drafted me, I figured it was a done deal. Then I discovered the company had a problem with me—my image was too clean. I didn't wear earrings or bling or have tattoos all over my body. They didn't use these words, but apparently I didn't fit their picture of what an African-American NFL player should look like. The contract didn't happen.

After my knee injury in 1989, I decided I needed to find another career option in case my playing days were about to end. The next year I founded Pro Moves, becoming the first African-American owner of a full-line shoe company. We had strong design, marketing, and sales teams, and a good product. Pro Moves took off. We sold a few million dollars' worth of shoes in stores such as Foot Locker, J. C. Penney, and Champs. We also had one of only three licenses granted by the NFL for players to wear our shoes.

In 1995, it appeared things had come full circle. The same company that rejected me at the beginning of my career called and asked for a meeting. They wanted to talk about the idea of transferring our NFL license over to them and have me represent them by wearing and endorsing their products.

As usual, I wore a suit to the meeting. It seemed to be going well. The company's marketing and public relations reps loved everything I, my brother, and my agent were saying. Before the meeting, they spoke in glowing terms about my business and positive reputation. Now, however, I was meeting the company president for the first time. I found it strange that he was so quiet. Finally, the marketing official turned to the president and said, "What do you think? You haven't said a word."

The president looked at me. In a stern voice, he said, "I do have something to say. Who are you?"

What? I wasn't sure what he was talking about. I tried to make a joke and stated the obvious: "I'm Tim Brown, Heisman Trophy winner and Pro Bowler."

The president didn't even smile. "I'm serious," he said. "I want to know who you are. Because you can't possibly be the successful person you're portraying here today. If I'm to believe everything I'm seeing and hearing, you could run my company if I let you."

Wow. It seemed this guy expected me to be the stereotype of an uneducated black athlete. Now I was steamed. I slammed the table with my hand and said, "What's wrong with that? If you think I'm coming in here trying to perpetrate a fraud to make a deal with you, you've got another thing coming. If you want to have me followed because you don't believe me, you're just going to be wasting your company's money."

That deal didn't happen either. Once again, my image didn't fit what this company, or at least this company president, had in mind. The next year, the firm signed another NFL player to a multiyear contract to wear their gear. An African-American player wearing baggy clothes and a lot more bling.

Was I angry about what happened? Yes. But I don't regret being true to myself. A man should be who he's meant to be.

———

The world exerts all kinds of pressure on each of us to conform to what everyone else is saying and doing. Peer pressure starts when we're young and never lets up. I certainly felt it with the Raiders. As I've said, I was able to resist the drinking and gambling and didn't do as well with the women and cursing. But at some point, a man needs to decide who he is and what he stands for. If he isn't sure, his environment will swallow him up.

Thanks to my upbringing, I knew that I shouldn't be cursing. I understood that it was wrong to use God's name in vain. I'd learned from the Bible about how I should speak: "Do not let any unwholesome talk come out of your mouths, but only what is helpful for building others up according to their needs" (Eph. 4:29). I'd never heard my mother swear, so I knew that abstaining from "unwholesome talk" was possible.

That doesn't mean it was or is easy. I still have to remind myself to give control of my thoughts and words to God. But it comes more naturally to me now that I'm again going to church consistently and reading my Bible regularly.

There was a time after I stopped swearing when the Raiders had a big game ahead. One of the players told me just before the start of the game that the team needed me to light a fire under them, to stand up in the locker room and curse them out. And I understood his point. I was tempted to do it—but I didn't. Instead, I said, "That's not me. That's not my role." If there were players on the team who admired the way I tried to live, how would I have any credibility with them if I suddenly jumped up and started acting like everyone else?

Marcus Allen always invites me to his annual celebrity golf tournament, which raises funds for charities. On the day before the golf tournament, he hosts a poker tournament as well, which includes some drinking and attracts beautiful women. I don't play poker, I don't drink, and I don't need to be around beautiful, available women. So the first time one of his representatives invited me, I said, "Hey, I'd love to play the golf, but I'm going to pass on the poker tournament. I'll come in that night and see the guys in the morning."

I have tremendous respect for Marcus. It's definitely not easy saying no to him. But the poker tournament wasn't and isn't who I am.

For the golf tournament, Marcus always finds beautiful women to drive the carts for the players. Every cart has one—except mine.

I've never asked Marcus to treat me differently than the other players. It's something I believe he does out of respect for me and the way I try to live. My golf teammates aren't always happy about it, but it's something I appreciate.

When I was thirty-three or thirty-four, people started saying that if I kept on putting up numbers like I was currently doing, I'd be a lock to enter the NFL Hall of Fame. I remember thinking, *Wow. The Hall of Fame. That would be incredible.* I definitely started getting excited about the idea.

As I prayed that week, however, I sensed God telling me something: *I didn't put you in this position so you can be a Hall of Fame player. I put you in this position so you can reach other folks and build My kingdom.* It was the same message I'd heard from Pastor Whitley all those years before. God was bringing me back to the truth. My life wasn't about glory for me, but glory for Him.

That's a challenge not only for celebrities but for anyone who inhales the sweet smell of success. Once we get a whiff of fame or wealth or power or adulation, we want more. We start to chase it. And if we're not careful, our thinking gets so warped that we completely lose sight of what we were created to be.

Ultimately, it doesn't matter how many football trophies, Oscars, or Grammys are on the shelf. The number of houses we own or stocks we've added to our portfolio isn't important. All of that stuff is meaningless. It's a foundation without substance, what the Bible calls "sinking sand." Family, friendships, and what we do to influence others for the better are so much more significant. And from my point of view, what matters most of all, the only things that last, are what we do for Jesus Christ.

I've learned that my purpose is to serve Him. That's who I am. That's who I'm meant to be.

14

SURROUND YOURSELF WITH GOOD PEOPLE

There is a friend who sticks closer than a brother.

PROVERBS 18:24

fter our awful 1997 season, Al Davis fired Joe Bugel and replaced him with the Philadelphia Eagles' offensive coordinator. At thirty-four, Jon Gruden became the youngest head coach in the NFL. He was only three years older than me.

Initially, I wasn't excited about the hire. I'd spoken up about wanting to see Art Shell take over again. He'd coached the Raiders from 1989 to 1994 and had the respect and support of the players. Al Davis had already expressed his regret over letting Art go. Since I had the choice to opt out of my contract that year, I thought seriously about leaving the Raiders when the announcement of our new coach was made. I didn't know anything about Jon Gruden.

I can't say I was overly impressed the first time I met him in a hallway at the Raiders offices. He wore a polo shirt, jeans, and running shoes. I acknowledged him and moved on. I had no idea who he was. He looked like an eighteen-year-old intern.

"So you're going to walk by your new head coach?" he said.

"Oh, man," I said, turning back to him. "Dude, you look younger than my son."

In our first sit-down meeting, Gruden asked me to stay in Oakland. "Just give me a shot," he said. "Give me one year to show you what it can be." He wanted to install a version of the West Coast offense that had been so successful for the 49ers and others.

I was still skeptical, partly because of what I'd seen before. Al Davis was famous for his hands-on approach to the Raiders. In recent years, that hadn't worked out too well. "Al's not going to let you do what you want to do with this offense," I said. "There's no reason for me to stick around and watch everybody fail."

"Look," Gruden said, "he's going to fire me in two years anyway. So I might as well do things my way."

He won me over. He was an intense football guy. He worked long hours every night and usually slept on a couch in the office. It was common to see him wearing the same clothes two days in a row. His enthusiasm was infectious, and watching him install plays on Wednesdays was like watching Mozart craft a masterpiece.

I also saw that either because he'd made an arrangement with Al or because he just ignored him, Gruden had more power than previous Raiders coaches. When looking for players, Al emphasized speed and tended to disregard everything else, but Gruden began bringing in guys who fit the style of football he wanted to play. Those people changed us for the better.

No one succeeds in life on his own. To achieve great things, you have to be around the right people. That's true in football and in life. In Jon Gruden, the Raiders found one of those people. They found another when they signed Eric Allen, a six-time Pro Bowler from New Orleans. Eric wasn't fast, but he was a smart, shut-down cornerback. Then we took cornerback Charles Woodson, the first primarily defensive player to win the Heisman, with the fourth pick of the 1998 NFL draft. Woodson made the Pro Bowl for us as a rookie.

In 1998, we doubled our win total from the season before, finishing with an 8-8 mark. Our record was the same the following year, but we added more important pieces. Rich Gannon was a thirty-three-year-old quarterback who'd been a backup, starter, and part-time starter for the Vikings, Redskins, and Chiefs. We signed him as a free agent. No one expected Gannon to dominate, but he was the perfect fit for our new offense. He passed for 3,840 yards in 1999 and made the Pro Bowl.

For that same season, we also signed a running back who hadn't found a home. Tyrone Wheatley had been traded from the Giants to the Dolphins, but Miami cut him during training camp. When our new fullback, Zack Crockett, broke his foot, we acquired Wheatley. It turned out to be another great move. Tyrone teamed with Napoleon Kaufman in the backfield and rushed for 936 yards, scoring eight touchdowns. In terms of overall yardage, we suddenly had the fifth-best offense in the NFL.

I stayed productive myself, making eighty-one catches for 1,012 yards in 1998 and ninety catches for 1,344 yards in 1999. I also made my eighth Pro Bowl in 1999.

What was exciting, though, was seeing the improvements in our team. The Raiders hadn't made the playoffs since 1993, when we were in Los Angeles. Oakland fans hadn't been treated to a Raiders playoff game since 1980, almost twenty years.

At last, thanks to the new people we were bringing in, we were poised to change that.

I've been fortunate throughout my life to so often be surrounded by good people. It started with my parents, brother, sisters, and extended family. You can't choose your relatives, so it's a blessing that I ended up with mine. As a professional athlete, you also don't usually have a choice in the people you work with. Coaches are hired by owners and management. Players are drafted, signed, traded, and released by a team's personnel officials—or as was often the case with the Raiders, by the owner. You can try to influence those decisions and hope you are heard, but for the most part you have to take the bad with the good.

Friends, though, are another matter. You get to choose the people you're close to. Those decisions are critical, because quality friends give you someone to confide in and get advice from, someone to share the good times with, and someone to rely on when you're in trouble.

I've been as blessed by my friendships as I have by my family. One of my best friends is a guy I've known since I was twelve years old. Marcus Camper went to a different middle school and high school, but like me he attended Victory Temple church. He became part of our group that played basketball after services, went to the Shake, Rattle, and Roll, and stopped to eat at the Bonanza restaurant. We thought those dinners at the Bonanza were the best in the world—all you could eat for $4.99. Come to think of it, the appeal might have been quantity more than quality.

Marcus was like me in a lot of ways. He played football and basketball. I never saw him drink or smoke. And he liked the girls. Marcus got married right after college. About the same time, he also gave his life to God. Now he lives just a mile down the road from me. Because our backgrounds are so similar, we have this ping-pong relationship—anything I bounce at him, whether it's a spiritual issue or a marriage issue, he understands and can bounce an answer right back. Most of the time, the answer is, "Brother, we are going to keep praying for that situation. We know God can work it out."

I can go on forever about Marcus. He's a man's man. He can fix anything, and if he doesn't get dirty doing it, he doesn't think it's worth doing. He's a Dallas police officer, the kind of guy who wouldn't hesitate to take a bullet for someone else. More important than that, he has what I'd almost call a beautiful spirit. Whenever he travels with me, he's like my sergeant at arms and bodyguard rolled into one. He'll update people who are waiting on me or stand next to me and answer questions if needed.

On top of all that, Marcus has this internal filter. Whatever happens to him, he processes it and what comes out always seems to be good while also honoring God. In so many ways, he's the man I aspire to be. It used to be that when he and I came out of church, kids would follow and ask for my autograph. I'd point to Marcus and say, "He's the one you should ask for an autograph. He's your example, not me." Just hanging out with him makes me a better man.

I've had other good friends and teammates who have also definitely influenced me for the better. Alvin Miller at Notre Dame. Marcus Allen and James Lofton with the Raiders.

And then there's Chester.

My first conversation with Chester McGlockton was before the 1992 season. Chester was a rookie defensive lineman. He was big. He was also cocky and gregarious. He'd tell everybody his plan for life, which was to play for six to eight years, retire, sit on his porch, and relax for the rest of his days.

I didn't care about all that. I was the Raiders' NFL Players Association representative at the time and it was my job to get information out to the team. I needed to make sure this rookie knew what was happening.

"Hey Big Rook," I said. "I need to get you to this meeting."

"I'm not coming to the meeting," Chester said.

"No," I said, "you're not hearing what I'm saying. I need you to be at this meeting."

Chester shook his head. "I'm not coming to the meeting."

"Brother, look," I said. "You can't be ignorant about what's going on with the Players Association and the league. I need you to—"

That was as far as I got. Chester jumped up and came at me, eyes on fire. Fortunately for me, Howie Long happened to be nearby, saw what was happening, and stepped in to slow Chester down. Chester had almost 150 pounds on me, so who knows if I'd still be alive to write this book if Howie hadn't been there.

"Big man, whoa," I said, my hands up.

"Don't be calling me ignorant!" Chester said.

"I didn't call you ignorant. I said you can't be ignorant of the situation here."

"Well, all I heard was me and ignorant."

That was our introduction. I ribbed Chester about it for a long time. Then we ended up playing a round of golf together. The more I talked to Chester, the more I realized he was really just a big teddy bear. We started playing golf and hanging out on off days. Not in the evenings, though. Chester liked to go drinking and I wasn't interested.

Then God started working on him. Chester met Zina, his future wife. Like me, he also went to Church of God in Christ, and we talked more and more about faith issues. Pretty soon, Chester was a changed man. When we both committed our lives to Christ in 1996, it created a stronger bond between us. In the offseason, we still talked two or three times a week. If he was anywhere near

Dallas or if I was anywhere in California, we'd meet somewhere. We might have looked like Laurel and Hardy together, but it was great. When he moved on to Kansas City in 1998, we made sure it didn't change our friendship.

Chester was important to me as a friend and as someone who encouraged me spiritually. When we talked about family, football, and the temptations that face an NFL player, he knew just where I was coming from. If he heard me talking or saw me acting in a way that he felt didn't line up with God, he let me know about it. My buddy Marcus is too nice to get in someone's face that way, but Chester wouldn't hesitate: "Boy, are you crazy? What is wrong with you?" He was always after me about treating my wife, kids, and extended family right. Yet I knew he wasn't judging me, that it was for my own good. And I often gave it right back to him.

A lot of men don't have friends like that—or if they do have them, they choose not to open the door to that kind of deep relationship. I can tell you, though, that sharing your problems and being accountable to a godly friend is a huge blessing. When you surround yourself with these kinds of people, you'll find it a whole lot easier to live a successful life.

———

Entering the 2000 season, the Raiders were also on the road to success. One of the keys was the last game of the 1999 season. We were on the road against Kansas City, where we always had problems. We hadn't won there in a decade. In terms of the postseason, the game didn't mean a thing to us, since we were 7-8. The Chiefs, on the other hand, needed a victory to take the division and make the playoffs.

We started as if we planned to roll over, giving up a punt return for a touchdown, an interception for a touchdown, and a field goal in the first quarter. There were times in the early Gruden years where in a situation like that, players felt the pressure to make a big play and tried to do too much. I was one of them. I might drift fifteen yards downfield instead of five or block the guy I thought was the biggest threat instead of who I'd been assigned to block. The intention was always good, but by giving up on the system and playing out of position, we sometimes messed up plays and hurt the team.

We didn't do that against Kansas City. We just kept fighting, trusted the system, and trusted each other. We came back to score three consecutive touchdowns in the second quarter, turning the game into a dogfight. With 1:39 left in the game, we were just past midfield, down by three points and facing a fourth-and-twelve. I lined up on the left side, faked as if I would cut outside, then ran hard on an angle toward the middle. Gannon's throw was perfect, low and between two defenders. I dropped to one knee for a twenty-yard gain. With fifty seconds left, Joe Nedney kicked a thirty-eight-yard field goal to tie the game. He connected again from thirty-three yards in overtime to give us a 41–38 victory.

That game showed us that if we believed in the system in place and in the people around us, we could beat anybody. It was our battle cry going into the next year.

We opened 2000 by squeaking by the Chargers, 9–6, then faced a tough test at Indianapolis. Peyton Manning had a big day, and the Colts dominated in the first half. They led after the first two quarters, 24–7. But once again, we fought back. It helped when our middle linebacker, Greg Biekert, ran off the field at halftime yelling, "I got it! I got it!" I didn't know what he was talking about until he met with the coaches. He'd figured out the sequence of numbers Manning was calling out before each play, at least enough to know if the play would be a run or pass. Our defense nearly shut out Manning and the Colts in the second half, forcing three turnovers, while Rich Gannon managed the offense superbly. We scored thirty-one straight points to win, 38–31.

A month later, we were 3-1 and found ourselves in another wild affair at San Francisco. It turned out to be one of my best performances as a pro. I caught a thirty-yard touchdown pass late in the third quarter and Gannon ran for a thirteen-yard score early in the fourth to give us a 28–14 lead. But the 49ers battled back with a pair of Jeff Garcia touchdown passes to tie the game at the end of regulation. In overtime, we missed a field goal, but Anthony Dorsett blocked one of theirs. On our next possession, we drove to the 49er thirty-one yard line.

I lined up in the left slot and went in motion to the right. I already had a couple of completions out of that formation by running up field three or four yards and turning for the catch. Their defender, Monty Montgomery, gave me a little less room each time. On this play, we faked the short pass and I ran long. Montgomery bit, expecting the short throw, and I was wide open for the game-winning score. I finished the game with seven catches for 172 yards and was named NFL Offensive Player of the Week.

We ended the season with a 12-4 record, easily winning the AFC West and earning a first-round bye in the playoffs. We hosted Miami in a divisional playoff. On the first Dolphin drive, Tory James intercepted a Jay Fiedler pass on our ten yard line and ran it back ninety yards for a touchdown. With our linemen controlling the game, Miami never challenged us, and we advanced with a 27–0 victory.

Our opponent in the AFC title game was the Baltimore Ravens. The winner would earn a spot in the Super Bowl. Although I'd played in one other AFC championship playoff back in 1990, we never really had a chance against Buffalo. This time we were favored to win. I was definitely excited about the chance to move on to the big game.

Unfortunately, it wasn't to be. Baltimore's defense smothered our offense and temporarily knocked Rich Gannon out of the game with a crushing hit in the second quarter. We trailed 10–0 at half-time. Gannon missed more time in the second half and all we could manage was a field goal. The Ravens beat us, 16–3.

I shed tears in the locker room. I was sure we were going to win that game. It was a terrible disappointment after a great year. When I exited the locker room, I felt broken. I had a hard time speaking.

Two young fans approached me. One, obviously noticing how distraught I looked, said, "Hey Tim, you going to be all right?"

As so often happened, my good friend and unofficial bodyguard, Marcus, was right next to me. When I hesitated, unable to speak, Marcus jumped in: "Of course he's going to be all right."

I was feeling anything but all right. Yet when Marcus said those words, it gave me another perspective. It gave me strength. I saw that as bad as it hurt, I would get through this. Marcus was like a pillar to lean on when I really needed one.

For Marcus, that moment was no big deal. But for me, it was an important turning point. It's just another example of what can happen when you're around good people.

15

RESPECT MUST
BE EARNED

The respect of those you respect is worth more
than the applause of the multitude.

ARNOLD GLASGOW

We went into the 2001 season full of optimism. We knew we had a good team and felt that an adjustment here and there was all we needed to compete for an NFL championship.

One adjustment the Raiders had to make that offseason was to replace running back Napoleon Kaufman, who retired to become a Christian minister. The back we signed as a free agent, a sparkplug named Charlie Garner, couldn't have been more different.

Charlie, five feet ten inches and 190 pounds, had gained over 1,100 yards in each of his previous two seasons with the 49ers. He was also vulgar and brash, the kind of guy who was never at a loss for words. When he found out about my faith, he was quick to let me know where he stood on the subject: "Yeah, you're one of these God guys. I know a whole bunch of you. I'll catch you later on. I know what's going to happen." He obviously believed I was saying one thing and living another.

There were moments throughout that season when he continued to try to needle me about my faith, usually in front of as many teammates as possible. I just ignored it. But in the locker room after a training camp practice the next season, Charlie came up to me and said quietly, "Okay, what's the difference between you and everybody else? I've heard a lot of God talk from guys, but you do it different."

"I can't speak for other guys or what they're doing," I said, "but I've made a decision to live for God. That's exactly what I'm doing." I explained about hearing some church people say when I was young that you couldn't play professional football and follow God. I felt otherwise. I told Charlie, "I'm determined to live this out to the fullest."

After that, Charlie started treating me differently. In fact, he made sure everybody else treated me different too. It started when we were on the road for a preseason game and I rode a hotel elevator down from my room. When the doors opened, the lobby was crammed with more than a hundred players and coaches, many listening to rap music, others yelling at each other to be heard. I didn't even have room to step off the elevator.

That's when Charlie jumped on top of a chair and bellowed, "Hey, hey, Mr. Brown is here! Cut all that nonsense out!"

The room went almost completely quiet.

"Why are you acting like Tim's the pope?" one player said. Charlie just glared at him. A path through the lobby opened up for me like the Red Sea did for Moses.

To me, what Charlie did was simply a sign of respect. He kept on doing it too. When I'd arrive at the locker room for practices or games, he'd yell out, "Turn that music off!" or "Hold up, Mr. Brown is coming through!" Though Charlie wasn't a believer himself, he saw that my words lined up with my actions. That was enough for him to give me VIP treatment.

Once I got established in the league, and especially after Marcus Allen left the team, my teammates started showing me respect in other ways. Mondays and Thursdays were my days to lift weights, which everybody knew. Everybody also knew that I preferred gospel music. So whenever I showed up at the weight room on those days, gospel was all that played. I didn't ask the guys to do that, but it was something I appreciated.

In the NFL, respect is everything. If you don't have the respect of your teammates, you're not going to be around very long. If you don't have the respect of your opponents, they'll try to take you down like lions preying on the weak members of a herd.

When I first joined the Raiders, I was an unknown quantity. Sure, everybody knew who I was because of the Heisman. But I hadn't done anything yet in the NFL. I had to earn that respect— primarily with my performance, but there were also times when I just had to stand up for myself.

One of those times was during a preseason practice at the start of my second year. Fred Biletnikoff had joined the Raiders as our wide receivers coach. Freddie is one of the NFL's all-time greats. A six-time All-Pro, he caught 589 passes in his fourteen-year career as a receiver with the Raiders and was a member of Oakland's American Football League championship team in 1965 and of the 1977 Super Bowl champions. In that game, he was named MVP. He's a Raiders legend.

He also has a legendary grasp of curse words, which I discovered during that preseason practice. We were working on the offense and I ran an incorrect route. I knew it before the play was even over. Freddie knew it too. As I walked back to the huddle, Freddie let me have it. He called me every swear word I'd ever heard and a few I hadn't.

As you might expect, many NFL coaches get on players to try to motivate them. It's fairly common practice. But it wasn't common to me. In all my years of football, from high school to college to my first year with the Raiders, no one had ever cussed me out like that. You also have to understand that, as Jon Gruden later pointed out to me, I can be a little sensitive. I respond well to encouragement, but not to someone trying to tear me down. Some guys need a coach to light a fire under them, but I'm already my own harshest critic. After Freddie lit into me, I had tears in my eyes for the rest of the practice.

Once the session was over, I quietly pulled my new coach aside. "Freddie," I said in my most polite voice, "if we're going to coexist, you can't talk to me like that. My daddy don't even talk to me like that. When I do something wrong, I usually know I've done wrong. If you dog curse me like that, I just shut down. That's just not going to be acceptable."

Freddie looked at me like I was crazy.

Later, he admitted he wasn't sure if I was nuts, if I was a wimp, or if I was serious. But he decided to give my approach a try. For the rest of that weekend he didn't say a word to me, and he saw that my play got better and better. Fred Biletnikoff was my coach for fifteen years, and not once after that day did he say anything out of line to me. When he was mad at all the receivers, he even made a point to leave me out of it. He'd swear at us till he was almost hoarse, then add, "Tim, I'm not talking to you."

I knew I had to talk to Freddie right away after he cussed me out. Part of it was from knowing who I am and what was going to help me be the best player I could be. The other part was about respect.

Next to winning, our primary focus when we step on the field is to earn the respect of teammates, coaches, and opponents. It isn't something that's handed to a player. You have to fight for it every day and every play, first to get it and then to keep it.

No amount of talking is going to matter. You hear plenty of trash talk in the NFL, but most of the time no one pays much attention. What matters is how you perform when the clock is running.

After a few Pro Bowls, I found I had that respect from opponents. When the other team identifies you as a player who needs to be stopped, that's a sign of esteem. For me, it sometimes meant that a defensive back got extra jacked up to put the hammer on me.

One of those times was a 1997 game in Seattle. Shawn Springs was a heralded rookie, the third player chosen in the draft. I'd watched him in college and knew he was talented. I think he wanted to establish his NFL reputation at my expense.

Before we even snapped the ball for our first play, Shawn was making lots of noise about what he'd do to me. I caught a short pass and when he made the tackle, he was pretty amped. I decided I needed to find out what I was dealing with. The next play was a run to my side of the field. I ran hard at first, then slowed down to give Shawn an angle on me. Sure enough, even though there was no need, he pushed me down at the end of the play. I didn't say a word.

Normally, I preferred to let my play speak for itself. I had no desire to resort to "extracurricular" activity on the field. But when you're challenged that way, you have to answer quickly. There are times when you literally have to fight for respect, and this was one of them.

The next play was another run in my direction. I came off the line slowly. Suddenly I jammed my helmet under Shawn's chin. He didn't like that a bit. As soon as he got loose, he pushed me. I grabbed his facemask and yanked his head down. With him trying to fight me and his head locked against me, I said, "Young buck, we can play this game any way you want. We can play like this or we can just play football. You make up your mind how we going to play this game today."

It took a couple of plays, but Shawn calmed down after that. We just played football. Like I've said, I tried to be a gentleman out there, but if I was physically challenged I responded. I wasn't going to let somebody push me around and run me out of the league.

My reputation got to the point where a few times I said to a defensive back, "Don't be trying to take me out. When you get a shot, you take it. I understand that. But don't try to hurt me or I'm going after your knees." Usually he was good with it. If I hadn't been a player with a few Pro Bowls under my belt, I never would have said that. Even if I had, they wouldn't have listened. The understanding I had with those guys was built on respect.

In a recent controversy in the NFL, New Orleans Saints players and coaches were suspended for an alleged program that provided bonuses for injuring opposing players and knocking them out of the game. In my day, bounties were a sign of respect. If you *didn't* have a bounty on your head it meant the other team didn't view you as a threat. Yes, there was money on the line, maybe five hundred dollars, maybe a little more. But as far as I knew, it didn't involve coaches and it wasn't about injuring another player to put him out of the game. It was about keeping Junior Seau from shooting the gap on runs and getting into the backfield or preventing Rodney Harrison from making a big hit. The idea was to stop the other team's top guys for that game.

Coaches say crazy things all the time to get players motivated before a game. Usually, that stuff goes in one ear and out the other. There's no way a coach could've talked me into intentionally hurting a player on another team. When I played, that was just not how it worked. The bounty existed because we respected that guy, not because we wanted to hurt him.

Raiders fans show their respect by being loyal and intense—and sometimes a little crazy. I remember one guy at an autograph show who was almost in tears when he got to me. He pulled up his shirt to reveal a tattoo of me catching a pass. That's intense.

Near the end of my career, some fans unveiled a new level of respect for me when they started calling me "Mr. Raider." I'd hear it after games when I came out of the locker room. There's really only one Mr. Raider—that's Jim Otto, the All-Pro center and original Oakland Raider who gave fifteen years on the field and really the rest of his life to the franchise. I hold the record for most regular-season games played by a Raider, 240, but when you add playoff games Jim is still top dog. Being compared to him is an honor that I appreciate to this day.

———

Respect is incredibly important to men, not just in the NFL but in all walks of life. We crave it from our peers, our friends, our family, and especially our girlfriends or wives. Plenty of authors have pointed out that most men would rather feel unloved than disrespected. There is a reason why the Bible tells husbands to "love your wives" (Eph. 5:25) while teaching that "the wife must respect her husband" (v. 33). For a man, respect is top priority.

As in the NFL, respect in everyday life isn't something you attract by talking about your accomplishments and intentions. It's earned by your actions. To me, sacrifice and respect often go hand in hand. You have to give up something to get respect. It might be letting go of the dream of buying the new car you've been eyeing so you can give that money to a needy neighbor. It might mean saying no to a promotion at work because it would take too much time away from your wife and family. It's making the tough, unselfish choices that benefit others.

If you're a dad and want to raise your kids right, sacrifice is definitely part of the deal. You might have to give up a few things and start spending your time and money on more family oriented priorities. To set an example for Taylor when he was younger, I listened only to gospel music. He didn't understand my position back then. He just rolled his eyes at me. But today, Taylor understands why I did it. I believe he respects me for it. In the long run, that sacrifice has been well worth it.

One thing I'm proud of is that when people compliment me nowadays, most often they talk about how I conducted myself off the field instead of how I played on it. They appreciate how I handled myself. My intention was never to earn people's praise, but it's rewarding to hear those comments. It's another by-product of respect.

To truly understand respect, we need to give it as well as pursue it. For me, that means acknowledging the one who deserves my respect above all others: God. The Bible says that "The fear of the LORD is the beginning of knowledge" (Prov. 1:7). Fear of the Lord is awe, reverence, love, and honor for Him all wrapped together. Some fear is healthy—we *should* be a little afraid of the dad who has authority over our earthly lives and the God who has authority over all of creation. Both have power that far exceeds our own.

It's pretty simple, actually. The reason people sometimes admire me is because of my respect for God. It's only because I worship and obey Him that anyone might find me worthy of respect.

———

As a wide receiver, when you talk about respect, you have to start with another of my new teammates for 2001: Jerry Rice.

To put it bluntly, Jerry is the greatest receiver in the history of the NFL. He might be the greatest player at any position. He holds the NFL records for most touchdowns, receiving touchdowns, receptions, receiving yards, and all-purpose yards. He was a thirteen-time Pro Bowler and ten times was named First Team All-Pro. He has won three Super Bowls and was a Super Bowl MVP.

When Jerry joined the Raiders as a free agent after sixteen years with the 49ers, he was thirty-eight years old and not quite the player he was in his prime. Raiders executive Bruce Allen called me before the signing was announced, asking for my opinion and if I'd have a problem playing with Jerry. He said I'd still be Jon Gruden's number one guy. "Look," I said, "if Jerry Rice can help get us to the Super Bowl, I don't care if I'm the number three guy. I just want to get to the Super Bowl." Little did I know that Jerry would play like he was twenty-eight, not thirty-eight.

Some reporters did predict that Jerry and I would have problems, that two stars at the same position couldn't coexist. That was ridiculous. I respected Jerry, and his comments to the media made it clear that he respected me: "Tim is the man here. He's the man. I'm just trying to play a significant part. For years I was the main focus. In a way, it feels good to be, not in a backseat mode, but not being the main guy."[1]

We showed right away that we would complement each other. In our season opener at Kansas City, we each made eight receptions, me for 133 yards and Jerry for 87, in a 27–24 victory. Our performance, and the whole team's, stayed strong. In November, we outlasted the New York Giants 20–10 to improve to 8-2.

Near halftime of that game, Jerry and I showed how dangerous we could be together. From our twenty-five yard line, Gannon completed a thirty-four-yard pass to Jerry. The next play, a five-yard pass to me, was called back by a penalty. Then Rich called out, "All Go Z Seam Special." I lined up in the slot on the right side, ran hard for ten yards, then made a move as if I was going outside. At the same time, Gannon pump faked to a receiver on the left. Instead of going outside, I headed for the post. After I ran another ten yards, Gannon hit me with a perfect pass, which turned into a forty-six-yard touchdown. Between me, Jerry, and Garner in the backfield as a rushing and receiving threat, opponents never knew which of us to cover.

With three games left, we led the AFC West with a 10-3 record. We stumbled down the stretch, losing our last three games, all close. Our 10-6 final record was still the best in the division, though it wasn't enough to earn a bye in the first week of the playoffs.

Despite losing to the Jets in the final game of the season, we held them off in the opening playoff round, 38–24. Our new additions were critical to the victory. Jerry caught nine balls for 183 yards and a touchdown, and Charlie Garner rushed for 158 yards on just fifteen carries. Garner's eighty-yard touchdown run down the right sideline with 1:40 left put the game away.

That set up a Saturday night confrontation with the New England Patriots in Foxborough, Massachusetts. They were led by a second-year quarterback who was essentially playing his first season: Tom Brady. The Patriots had won eleven of the fourteen games Brady started, including the last six in a row. This was his first playoff test. It turned out to be a battle in a blizzard.

We knew earlier that week that snow was in the forecast. Most of the guys figured it was the worst thing that could happen, that it would slow us down and nullify our speed. Personally, though, I never minded playing in bad weather. I was used to it from my Notre Dame days because the university didn't have an indoor practice facility. If the field was slippery, I thought it was to my advantage since I knew where I was going and the defender didn't.

Sure enough, we played that game in a snowstorm, with a wind chill of eighteen degrees. Mostly because of the weather, neither side could make much happen offensively in the first half. The lone score was a thirteen-yard touchdown pass from Gannon to James Jett in the second quarter. We outscored New England in the third quarter too, kicking a pair of field goals to their one to take a 13–3 lead.

I got hurt in the middle of that quarter. I was running a quick slant and a pass came low and behind me. When I tried to slow down and reach back to make the catch, Ty Law hit me on my right shoulder. I didn't know it then, but I'd suffered a tear in my groin, what they call a sports hernia today. My leg went numb for a while, but it got better and I played the rest of the game without any problems. The ironic thing is that I needed time to heal after that game. If we'd won, I wouldn't have been able to play in the AFC championship or the Super Bowl, which would have been devastating.

The nightmare that still plagues many Raiders fans—and players—began early in the fourth quarter. We fumbled a punt for the second time in the quarter, Brady connected on nine consecutive passes, and then he ran up the middle for a six-yard touchdown. With 7:57 to play in the game, our lead was only 13–10.

We'd been waiting all day for this young quarterback to make a mistake. With 1:50 left in the game and the Patriots driving on our forty-two yard line, it finally happened—only it didn't count.

It's become one of the most famous plays in NFL history. Brady drops back to pass. Charles Woodson blitzes and hits Brady. The ball comes loose. Greg Biekert recovers. It's ruled a fumble and Oakland ball. We celebrate and our offense starts going onto the field. The referees go to instant replay for what seems to be the longest referee review ever. They finally cite an obscure rule installed just two years before, saying that Brady's arm had been moving forward and that he then tried to tuck it toward his body. It's not a fumble but an incomplete forward pass. New England ball. (In 2013, the "tuck rule" was deleted from the rulebook—about time!)

The rest of that night is a bad memory. Adam Vinatieri kicks a forty-five-yard field goal with thirty-two seconds left to tie the game. New England wins the overtime coin toss and receives the ball first. The Patriots drive down the field, Vinatieri kicks another field goal, and just like that, the game is over.

To say that game left a bad taste in our mouths would be the understatement of the century. It was the quietest locker room I've ever been in. We were in mourning. For a long time, we had felt disrespected by the NFL and its officials. The sense was that because of Al Davis's many conflicts with the league, we were always eleven against twelve, with that twelfth man being an official. When year after year the Raiders were at or near the top in team penalties, it was difficult to not think that way. The game against the Patriots felt like the culmination of all that. As an emotional Gruden said when he stood before us in the locker room after it was over, "They are never going to let you win."

As crushing as that loss was, we walked away from it with more respect for the Patriots and for Brady. The truth was, they'd taken advantage of the opportunities given to them and the kid had played good football. I wasn't shocked when they went on to win the Super Bowl.

As the years passed, respect would grow for the Patriots, for Coach Bill Belichick, and for Brady. No one handed it to them. They went out and earned it. That's the way it should be.

16

LITTLE THINGS LEAD TO BIG RESULTS

Little by little does the trick.

AESOP

I was shocked and disappointed when just a month after our loss to the Patriots in January 2002, Tampa Bay announced that it had traded four draft picks and $8 million to us for Jon Gruden. I don't think Al Davis wanted to pay Gruden what he would probably ask for when his contract expired in a year. Jon decided it was time to go and Al let him.

In hindsight, I shouldn't have been surprised. Gruden's comment to the team in Foxborough that the NFL would "never let you win" was a hint. I think he'd had enough of the battles with Al and was ready to leave.

Our offensive coordinator, Bill Callahan, was named head coach. I didn't see it as an inspiring choice, but I also felt it could have been worse. Callahan was generally a good strategy guy who unfortunately had a way of rubbing players the wrong way, sometimes talking in a condescending manner. On the other hand, he gave us continuity. We didn't have to learn new plays and a new system. We knew we already had a good team, so big changes weren't necessary. If we just focused on doing the little things right, victories would follow.

Success in the NFL depends on many factors. Talent, speed, physical strength, and conditioning are part of it. So are intelligence, teamwork, and confidence. What so often brings all these together, though, is consistently doing the small things that lead to positive, long-term results.

For me, for example, that meant lining up in the exact same stance for every play. When I first got to the Raiders, James Lofton showed me how he always started by holding his arms up in front of him, almost like a boxer, fists closed. It meant he was ready to do battle with or push off from a defensive back the instant the ball was snapped. I decided to adopt the same technique. It's not that common in the NFL. Most receivers probably think it doesn't look cool. But it meant I didn't waste an extra half second bringing my arms up after the play started—a small thing that sometimes paid off in a big way.

One good thing the coaches did that season was to give more control of the offense to Rich Gannon. By the end of the season, they were sending four plays to the huddle, two runs and two passes, and then Rich called one of the four at the line of scrimmage. It wasn't like an audible, where the defense usually knows we're changing the play and can switch at the last moment to a new formation. Instead, Gannon could quickly scan how the defense was set up and choose the most effective of our four options. Because of Gannon's experience and because he was so smart and well prepared, it worked great. It was another seemingly small decision that made us more successful.

We opened 2002 with a 31–17 victory over Seattle. Then we traveled to Pittsburgh to take on the Steelers. We discovered early in the game that when we lined up in what we called Trio Left East, with me in the slot and Jerry Rice outside, the Steelers showed before the play if they were blitzing or not. We could tell because if I went wide enough, the defender wouldn't move with me because he wanted to stay close enough to reach the quarterback. If the Steelers showed blitz, my response was automatic. When the play started, I'd drop back a step, run a little semicircle, and Gannon would fire the ball to me in almost the exact spot where I'd started. It was good for seven or eight yards every time.

I always lined up with my feet staggered, left foot in front. For most plays, I also put my weight on my left foot. That had me in the best position to quickly accelerate for a catch or block. But on those plays that countered the Pittsburgh blitz, I shifted my weight to my back foot. I couldn't move my body or it would tip off the defender, but by subtly transferring my weight, it gave me just a little more time to separate from the defense and make the catch.

We kept running that same formation against the Steelers and Rich kept finding me or someone else with short passes. Gannon finished with 403 yards passing. His forty-three completions, on a whopping sixty-four attempts, was an NFL record for a non-overtime game. Jerry had eleven receptions for ninety-four yards and I had seven catches for sixty-three yards. Once again, the little things added up. By winning that game 30–17 against a tough Steelers team on the road, we knew we had the potential for another big year.

We won our first four games, then hit a rough patch and lost the next four, two of them in overtime. We turned it around against

Denver, stopping the Broncos 34–10. Rich set another NFL record with twenty-one consecutive completions in that game. The next week we got some revenge against the Patriots, defeating them 27–20. In that game I passed Gene Upshaw to set the record for regular season games played for the Raiders.

After a season that included ninety-one receptions for 1,165 yards, I'd been selected to my ninth Pro Bowl in 2001. Now I was thirty-six years old and in my fourteenth season—not bad considering I once thought I'd be lucky to play until I was thirty. All those little things I'd been doing over the years had added up. Going into a December 2 game against New York in front of a nationwide *Monday Night Football* audience, I had 996 career receptions. In the history of the NFL, only Jerry Rice and Cris Carter had more.

I made three catches in the first half, two for twenty yards, but our offense was out of sync. We trailed 10–6 when we got the ball in the third quarter and drove to New York's thirty-two yard line.

When you dream of a historic moment like your one thousandth catch, you imagine making a leaping grab over a defender or making a spectacular move to break free in the end zone for a touchdown. That isn't what happened for me. I ran a little slant to the middle, Rich didn't see an open receiver to the left, and he dumped it off to me instead. I was tackled right away after a six-yard gain. But maybe that was appropriate. My success had been built just as much on being steady and doing the little things right than on making eye-popping plays.

I didn't think anyone from my family was at the game to help me celebrate. Sherice was nearly seven months pregnant, so I knew she was home resting. But the Raiders put one over on me. They'd flown Taylor; my daughter Timon; Sherice's mother, Joanne; my brother; all four of my sisters; and three nieces to the game. The biggest surprise was that they'd also flown out my parents. My dad always recorded my NFL games on TV, but he didn't attend them in person. Mama had never watched me play in person at any level. In my twenty-seven years of football, this Monday night game was the only one Mama ever attended. She still didn't like the violence and still was afraid of seeing me get hurt.

They stopped the game after my catch, and while players and staff congratulated me, they drove Mama, Dad, Timon, and Joanne onto the field in a golf cart. As you can imagine, it really got emotional for me when I saw Mama. I hugged everybody, then walked to that big Raiders shield in the middle of the field. I waved to the crowd with the football I'd just caught. I wanted to thank them for all the support over the years. The roar they gave me back was amazing. I had to wipe away the tears as I walked off the field.

The break in the action must have helped us. We scored on a twenty-six-yard touchdown pass to Jerry Rice on the very next play.

Later in that contest, which we won 26–20, I went over fourteen thousand receiving yards for my career and passed my old teammate James Lofton to rank number two all-time, again behind Jerry. I had come a long way from the playground at Mount Auburn Elementary where I'd first played the game.

———

An author and congressman named Bruce Barton once wrote, "Sometimes when I consider what tremendous consequences come from little things, I am tempted to think there are no little things."[1] I believe he's right. By themselves, the small things we do every day to make life better for ourselves and the people around us don't seem to amount to much. But when we apply them consistently over days, weeks, months, and years, the effect is powerful.

One of the things I'm most proud of about my NFL career is

that other than my second year, when I had the knee injury, the only practice I missed was a single day in 2001 when my father had heart surgery. In my sixteen years with the Raiders, I missed just one game, in 1992 after a hamstring injury. Even then, I still made every practice that week. I could have played if they'd let me.

Would it have been a major news event if I'd sat out a practice to rest sometime during my career? No. In most people's eyes, one practice is a small thing. But I was committed to doing those small things right, each and every time. When you start putting them together year after year, you get excellence and consistency.

Success in the business world depends just as much on mastering the little things. In fact, that's exactly the advice my father gave me when I first moved into the shoe business. "Dad," I told him, "we've got this deal going where we're going to make three million a month."

"Mm hm," he said. "You know, you don't need to worry about making the big money. Just make the little money. If you make enough of the little money, guess what? It adds up to the big money."

Three months later, I saw his point more clearly. "Hey," my dad said, "what happened to that deal y'all had?"

"Well," I said, "it didn't pan out."

"Oh, okay," he said. He waited a moment. I squirmed a little because I knew what was coming. Finally, he got to it. "Did I tell you that you don't need to go after the big money? Just keep making the little money." I listened closer this time because I realized he was right. My dad, in fact, put us in touch with one of our best clients, a firm that never placed big shoe orders but consistently made small ones. Dad would ask me, "How's Roberts Ready to Wear doing?"

"Great," I'd say. "They bought 250 pairs of shoes this month."

"And how's that other big deal doing?"

I'd shake my head and my dad would just laugh.

Consistency in the little things is also incredibly important to a marriage and family. You can't be wishy washy. You've got to say what you do and do what you say, time after time. Sherice knows me well enough that if she takes a call from someone inviting me to an event where alcohol is going to be a major feature, she tells the caller I won't be coming. She doesn't have to ask me because I've been consistent about that throughout our years together.

If you're a parent, you better believe your kids are looking for you to be consistent. They'll call you on it in an instant if you're not. Our daughter Timon is fifteen. Like me, she's quiet. She's also smart and athletically gifted. And like a lot of kids in their early teens, she has a full schedule of activities. It would be easy for us to let her skip Sunday or Wednesday church once in a while to accommodate everything else she's doing. It would be just a "little thing." But we don't do that. Unless someone is seriously ill, we're always there as a family. Consistency in the little things, particularly when it relates to God, is important to me as a father.

The small things are vital to a thriving spiritual life. Sherice is especially good about making time daily for Bible reading and prayer. When I'm consistently talking with God and studying His Word, I definitely notice the difference in my life. Taking even five or ten minutes every day to connect with God will keep your relationship with Him going.

The way we pay attention to the little things tells a lot about our character and commitment to following the Lord. In the Bible, Jesus says, "Whoever can be trusted with very little can also be trusted with much" (Luke 16:10). In the context of the passage, He was talking about how we handle money, but His point also applies to more than that. If we honor God in small ways, He's more likely to bless us with greater opportunities to bless Him in large ways. That's when life really gets exciting. Today, I believe that's a big reason He allowed me so much success in the NFL. I'm still trying to use that blessing to honor Him.

———————

The Raiders finished the 2002 season with an 11-5 record, winning seven of the last eight games. In many ways it was a year of triumph for us. Our offense led the league in total yardage, and our defense was sixth in points allowed. Rich Gannon had an incredible year and was named the NFL's Most Valuable Player. Charlie Garner totaled 962 rushing yards and another 941 receiving yards. Jerry Rice, forty years old at the end of the season, made ninety-two catches for 1,211 yards and was named to his thirteenth Pro Bowl. I was second on the team with eighty-one receptions and 930 yards, breaking my streak of nine consecutive years with over a thousand yards.

We opened against the Jets in the playoffs. They stayed with us in the first half, battling to a 10–10 tie. But our defense stepped up in the second half. They shut out New York while Jerry Porter had a huge game for us with six receptions for 123 yards and a touchdown. We beat the Jets, 30–10.

That put us back in the AFC championship for the game against the Titans, which we won 41–24. Finally, all the years of sacrifice and trying to do the little things right paid off. At last, I would realize the dream of every player who ever steps onto a football field. I was going to the Super Bowl.

17

A MAN KNOWS HIS PRIORITIES

If you continually ask yourself "What's important
now?" you won't waste time on the trivial.

LOU HOLTZ

uper Bowl XXXVII would be played on January 26, 2003, in
San Diego's Qualcomm Stadium. For one of the rare times in
NFL history, the league allotted only one week between the conference championships and the big game. Those days just before and
after the game were among the weirdest, most wonderful, and most
memorable of my life.

We flew from Oakland to San Diego on Monday. We had a light
practice Tuesday, which was followed by pictures and interviews
with a huge media contingent. I had more than football and the
media on my mind, however. Sherice was back home in Dallas, eight
and a half months pregnant with twins, a boy and a girl. Between

the pregnancy, my one thousandth catch, and the chance to win a Super Bowl, I couldn't ask for more. As someone told me, "God decided to shine on you all at one time."

The only problem was that the babies could come at any moment. There'd been talk of Sherice and her doctor flying in for the game, but after her appointment Tuesday, the trip was deemed too risky. That night, Sherice had some major contractions and thought labor had started. It turned out to be a false alarm. I wished I could be home rubbing Sherice's belly or that she could be with me, but I knew she was in good hands. Fortunately, I've always had the ability to tune out what's going on around me and focus on the immediate. It was time to concentrate on football.

Our opponent in the Super Bowl would be the Tampa Bay Buccaneers, the team Jon Gruden had been traded to just a year earlier. They were still largely the great defensive team that previous coach Tony Dungy had put together. Tampa Bay had knocked out Philadelphia in the NFC championship game, 27–10.

We had the NFL's top offense and the Bucs had the league's top defense. Tampa Bay was also number one in pass defense but not quite as strong against the rush, at number five. Since the Buccaneer defense was so fast and quick, and since our offensive line averaged about 330 pounds and their defensive line averaged about 275 pounds, the coaches decided to focus on our power running game. The plan was to wear Tampa Bay down early in the game, then go to the air later. On Wednesday and Thursday, we practiced packages that featured running back Tyrone Wheatley and fullback Zack Crockett.

It made a lot of sense to me. When we lined up in a short-yardage, "heavy-package" formation—usually a running play featuring two tight ends and just one wide receiver—Jerry Porter was our primary receiver. I knew I wouldn't play much while we pounded them with our running game. I didn't care about that. I just wanted that Super Bowl ring.

On Friday morning, however, everything changed. When we got to practice, Bill Callahan announced that we had a new game plan. "We're going to throw the ball sixty times on these guys," he said. "This is what we do. This is how we got here. We can make it happen."

I didn't like the sound of this a bit. Yes, we had the NFL's top passing offense. We were very good at what we did, no doubt about it. But we were successful because we were smart. If a team couldn't stop our passing game, we passed. If they couldn't stop our running game, we ran. In Charlie Garner, Wheatley, and Crockett, we definitely had weapons on the ground.

More important, the last-minute change put a lot of pressure on Rich Gannon and our offensive line. One of Gannon's greatest strengths was his ability to prepare for an opponent. He studied them and the game plan until he knew just what they were going to do and just what he wanted to do. Now, in the most important game of his life, he suddenly had to speed up his routine big-time.

The other guy under big pressure from the change was center Barret Robbins. He was responsible for reading the defense and calling out blocking assignments even before Gannon walked up to the line. It had been a great season for Barret. He was a first-team All-Pro. But now he, too, was expected to make a major adjustment just two days before the Super Bowl.

As one of the team leaders, I felt I needed to say something to Bill Callahan. As we walked off the field at the end of the Friday practice, I caught up with him. "Bill, why are we doing this?" I said. "Why change now?"

"Hey, we can handle it," he said. "We've handled it all year."

That didn't really answer my question. But from our brief

conversation, I could tell he was determined to stick with the new plan. There didn't seem to be much more to say.

Barret Robbins also talked to Bill Callahan at the end of that practice. As best as I remember, he said, "Do not do this to me. I don't have time to make my calls, to get my calls ready. You can't do this to me on Friday. We haven't practiced full speed, we can't get this done."

Bill's answer was brief: "It'll be fine. You'll be okay."

It wasn't until we got to the locker room the next morning that we heard Barret was missing. Then word circulated that he'd been found after having partied in Tijuana, Mexico, the night before. At that point we thought he had been drunk but would still be able to play. Saturday night, though, the word was that he was in the hospital. That's when we realized Barret wouldn't play at all. We'd be going with Adam Treu, who was a solid reserve, but expecting him to replace one of the top centers in football in the Super Bowl on one day's notice? That was ridiculous.

Even before that weekend, the players and coaches knew Barret was dealing with some personal issues. No one can say for sure, but it seemed to me that the switch in game plan could have pushed him over the edge. It wasn't until later that we learned about his bipolar disorder and more of the details of his wild night in Tijuana. Today, Barret says he remembers almost nothing from that weekend.

I don't seek out controversy when I'm interviewed or when I do my radio and television work, but I don't avoid it either. I just try to be honest. I've commented on the mistakes made that weekend in 2003 many times over the years, but it wasn't until just before the 2013 Super Bowl that the media really picked up on it. At the time of the Super Bowl against Tampa Bay, many of the Raiders players, including me, called what Callahan did that week sabotage. I used that word again in 2013, which is what made all the headlines. The story got even more life when Jerry Rice backed up my comments.

From my perspective, it had long seemed that Bill Callahan didn't want to be with the Raiders and that he didn't like his players. Twice he'd walked off the field on us before games had ended. He was good friends with Jon Gruden. He'd unnecessarily made it much harder on his team, especially his quarterback and center, by switching game plans on us at the last minute. Many people say that was simply a bad coaching decision. A few have suggested it was orders from Al Davis. To me, as outrageous as it sounds, it seemed Bill was either consciously or unconsciously trying to lose. Of course, I can't say for certain what was going through his mind. It's just my opinion based on what I saw. Would we have won if we'd stuck to the original plan, been more prepared, and had Barret with us? Who knows? I'm not trying to take anything away from Tampa Bay. They put on a great performance. But could it have been a much better game? Of that I have no doubt.

Despite all the drama leading up to kickoff, I was determined to put it out of my mind and do everything I could to win—and to appreciate the moment. While we waited for the referees and the coin toss, I did a slow, 360-degree turn, taking in the sights and sounds of the stadium. I noticed in huge letters on the scoreboard the words "God Bless America." Suddenly the scoreboard switched its message so that it read "America Bless God." I'd never seen that before. It was a nice reminder for me that even though millions were watching around the world, I wasn't here for personal glory. Some things were more important than even the Super Bowl. Soon enough, I would need that perspective.

We got off to a promising start. Charles Woodson intercepted a Brad Johnson pass on Tampa Bay's opening drive and I caught a nine-yard pass for a first down. The drive stalled when Gannon was sacked, so Sebastian Janikowski kicked a field goal that gave us a 3–0 lead.

Tampa Bay came back to tie it with a field goal of its own. Our next possession consisted of two incomplete passes and another quarterback sack. When we stopped the Buccaneers and got the ball back, the coaches told us we were returning to a running attack. Now we weren't sure what the game plan was. A pair of Zack Crockett runs got us six yards, we threw an incomplete pass, and Tampa Bay had the ball again. Our defense held, but from that point on, the game snowballed on us.

It started to unravel late in the first quarter when Dexter Jackson intercepted a Gannon pass after we'd moved into Tampa Bay territory. That led to a second-quarter field goal to give Tampa Bay momentum and the lead. On our next drive, Jackson made another interception and returned it twenty-five yards to give the Bucs great field position. They scored a touchdown and had a 13–3 advantage.

Once again, our offense didn't do much. We punted, and Tampa Bay drove the length of the field for another touchdown. Incredibly, we were down 20–3 at the half. It hadn't helped that the Buccaneers were familiar with the terminology for many of our play calls. Much of that was a carryover from the year before when Jon Gruden was still with us.

Any thoughts we had of a comeback were quickly crushed in the third quarter. We gave up the ball after two short passes and an incompletion on our opening drive. Brad Johnson led the Bucs on an eighty-nine-yard drive for a touchdown. Two plays later, Gannon was intercepted again. Dwight Smith ran the ball back forty-four yards for a touchdown. We were down 34–3. We still had more than a quarter to play, but the game was over.

The final score was 48–21. Rich Gannon had thrown a career-high five interceptions in forty-four passing attempts. Three of the interceptions were returned for Tampa Bay touchdowns. The nine-yard catch on our opening series was my only reception on the day. Any way you looked at it, the Super Bowl was a disaster for the Raiders.

As disappointing as the game was, I was quickly reminded of more important matters. After spending ten or fifteen minutes on the field congratulating the Buccaneers, I entered the locker room. Raiders official Marc Badain said, "Tim, the doctor called. They're trying to hold on with your wife, but you need to get there ASAP. We've got a jet for you ready to go."

That jet was one of the coolest things the Raiders ever did for me. What's funny about it now is that we had an arrangement with Jimmy Kimmel and ABC. If we'd won the game, I was supposed to get on a helicopter, still wearing my uniform, and fly to L.A. to do a live interview on the show with Jimmy. Maybe it's a blessing we lost. I can't see me calling Sherice and saying, "Honey, can you hang on just a little longer? I've got to do a show on TV."

I stayed in the locker room for interviews, but my answers were pretty curt. Now that the game was over, my focus was on getting back to Oakland to be with my wife. After a quick shower, I was out the door.

In no time, the jet carried me, Timon, and Sherice's mom to Oakland. We were whisked to Alta Bates hospital, where we arrived just before midnight. Minutes later, I was in scrubs and in the delivery room with Sherice, watching the doctors go to work on a C-section. At 12:23 a.m., our daughter Tamar was born, followed two minutes later by Timothy. I was thrilled.

The doctors checked the babies out, pronounced them both healthy, and wrapped them up. Nurses wheeled Sherice to the recovery room and I followed, carrying one newborn in each arm.

A nurse approached me in the hallway and said, "Oh, I'm so sorry about what happened tonight."

I stared at her. "Ma'am, I don't know what you're talking about," I said.

She raised her eyebrows. "The Super Bowl," she said.

"Oh, yes, okay," I said. "Thank you." I'd already put the game out of my mind. As excited as I was about finally standing on the NFL's brightest stage, as upset as I was about the problems and changes that led up to the game, as disappointed as I was about the outcome, none of it mattered to me then. What mattered were the two beautiful new lives that had been entrusted to our care, both of them now blinking up at me as I held them for the first time. No football setback could spoil the joy of that moment.

———

Gale Sayers, the great Chicago Bears running back, once wrote a book called *I Am Third*. The title was based on a placard he'd seen on his college track coach's desk. The coach said it reminded him that "The Lord is first, my friends are second, and I am third." Beginning with his second year in the NFL, Sayers started wearing a medallion that read "I Am Third."

I would amend the wording of that phrase slightly so that it reads "my friends *and family* are second," but I completely agree with its meaning. To be successful in life, a man has to have his priorities in order. You see plenty of guys struggle because they get the order wrong and put their own needs at the top. For a lot of years I was one of those guys, and sometimes I still don't get it right. But I think I'm doing better.

The key to it all, of course, is keeping God at the forefront. I don't know how people make it in this world without God in their life. My mom and I talk about this all the time. Each of us is continually bombarded by illness or conflicts with friends or a job loss or the heartache of losing a loved one. God is our comfort and our guide through it all, the one constant in a swirling sea.

I remember a moment in the season after the Super Bowl. Jerry Rice was furious, stomping around on the practice field after Callahan had chewed him out. I followed behind. He suddenly stopped and said to me, "How do you do this?" I knew it wasn't a football question but a life question.

"Jerry, I gave my life to Christ seven years ago," I said. "Everything I do, everything I say, every decision I make is for Him. I'm not 100 percent consistent with it, but when I'm about to go off on somebody, I always try to remember who I'm representing. That's just where I am, man."

I like to keep it simple. When I follow and serve God and give Him the credit for whatever blessings He allows me to have, everything else seems to line up. That's what helps me keep life in perspective.

Family has a way of putting things in perspective too. Back in 1998, our first daughter was due in late September, but our doctors informed us that Timon would be at least six weeks premature. Sherice and I were both worried. Would there be complications? Would she live a healthy, normal life?

When Timon did arrive six weeks early, she weighed just five pounds, nine ounces. I knew it wasn't routine when about ten doctors gathered around our new baby right after her birth. I didn't realize I could love someone I'd known only five minutes so much. Timon was immediately placed in the Neonatal Intensive Care Unit. The doctors were concerned about weight loss, bilirubin, and jaundice. Everything turned out fine, but it was a fearful time.

Timon wasn't the only one I worried about. Sherice lost a lot of blood during the delivery. When she got out of bed for the first time, a doula was there to help her walk. I was in the next room. Suddenly I heard a panicked voice: "Mr. Brown! Mr. Brown!"

I rushed in to see Sherice sitting down, her eyes rolling to the back of her head. I was scared. The only thing I knew to do was grab her, shake her, and yell, "Jesus!" I did that three times. Not a very eloquent prayer, but I knew He'd understand.

On that third exclamation, Sherice snapped out of it and seemed fine again. It turned out she was dehydrated. She recovered without further complications, but once again, I'd briefly confronted the frightening possibility of losing someone I loved so dearly. When something like that happens, it reestablishes priorities real quick. Maybe that's one reason why God allows us to go through so many tough moments. It forces us to see what truly matters.

———

The Raiders nearly reached the mountaintop during our run to the Super Bowl in 2002, but in 2003 we fell fast and hard. Rich Gannon got hurt in our seventh game and didn't play the rest of the season. We lost five consecutive games in the middle of the year, four of them by a touchdown or less. Bad feelings between Bill Callahan and the players increased, with our head coach at one point calling us "the dumbest team in America" on national TV. We ended the season 4-12, tied for the worst record in the NFL. Callahan was fired and replaced by Norv Turner.

As a team, we struggled badly on offense and defense in 2003. With Gannon out, my numbers also dropped dramatically. My fifty-two receptions for 567 yards were my lowest totals since 1992. Our team had gotten older, all of a sudden it seemed, but no way did I think I was done. I was excited about coming back in 2004 and showing that we were better than what our terrible 2003 indicated.

I saw Al Davis at our mandatory minicamp in June 2004. He asked about my plans for the future. "Mr. Davis," I said, "I'm committed through this year. Quite frankly, I don't know how much longer I want to play after that. I'd like to see how it goes." That seemed fine with Al. We talked about me mentoring Jerry Porter in the upcoming season.

Two weeks before training camp, however, Al left me a phone message. It was the first time he'd called me in my sixteen years with the Raiders. All he said when I called back was that we would talk at training camp. That sounded ominous. I told Sherice not to pack anything for camp.

At camp, though, I suited up and practiced with the team that first day. I decided I'd been overreacting. If they wanted to get rid of me, I figured, they would have cut me right away. Al must have had something else he wanted to discuss with me.

At breakfast the next morning, I was informed that Al wanted to see me. My fears quickly returned when he said, "We have a problem." He told me the coaches felt I was uncoachable, that I had too much influence in the locker room. When a coach told the players something, they looked to me to nod or shake my head. I'd memorized every offensive play in our playbook so that I could help other players with the new system. That, Al said, was also a problem.

I agreed that I was a team leader, but I reminded Al that I'd used my influence to help the organization, not tear it down. That didn't seem to matter. The Raiders wanted to offer me a package where I'd play against only the other AFC West teams.

"Mr. D," I said, "you're offering me that package because you know I'm not going to accept it. You want to be able to say, 'We wanted Tim to stay but he walked away.' I can't go into the locker room and tell them, 'Hey guys, I'm just going to play in six games this year.' So are we saying this is the end?"

Al wanted to talk with the coaches again. They kept me away from the other players for the rest of that day, bringing meals to a separate room. Rich Gannon came by to find out what was going on but there was little I could say.

By the next morning, nothing had changed. We held a press conference announcing that after sixteen years with the Raiders, I'd been released.

Talk about tough. I cried at the press conference and I cried again on the drive home as I listened to the radio replay of the press conference. Sixteen years was a long time, nearly half my life. I'd tried to give my best to my teammates and the organization every day. It was hard to believe that my time with the Raiders, and maybe my football career, was over. Since my knee injury I'd always been mentally prepared to leave the game, but this wasn't the way I wanted to go out.

It wasn't easy to picture myself in another team's uniform, but there was one place I thought I might be comfortable: Tampa Bay. Jon Gruden knew me and what I could do. They'd also signed former Raiders such as my good friend Rickey Dudley, Charlie Garner, and Matt Stinchcomb. Even Bruce Allen, the former Raiders executive, was there. When my agent told the Buccaneers I was interested in continuing my career there, it didn't take long to make a deal. Sherice and I leased a house in Tampa and moved the kids and all our Oakland furniture across the country.

It turned out to be a rough season. I played a lot early in the year, and even scored my one hundredth career touchdown in Oakland on a sixteen-yard pass to the back of the end zone. The Raiders fans were great to me, giving me an ovation before the game and again when I scored. But we lost that game, part of four consecutive losses to open the season. The Tampa fans unleashed their frustration against us ex-Raiders. They felt the team had become "Raiders East," and because it wasn't working, they weren't happy. I remember making a fifteen-yard reception in one home game and getting booed.

Also, as players recovered from injury and the coaches worked in young receivers, my playing time diminished. During the last home game of the year, an unusually cool afternoon, I caught an eight-yard pass in the opening series and then sat on the bench. With five or six minutes left in the game, receiver Michael Clayton took a hard hit and I was suddenly back in. On the first play, with no time to warm up, I had to fight through an inside defender and run a post route. I nearly pulled every muscle in my body. On the way back to the huddle I thought, *Are you crazy? Are you really going to kill yourself trying to stay on the football field? You can't play football like this.*

I finished the season with twenty-four receptions for two hundred yards. It was clear to me that my time in Tampa was done.

After the season, both New England and Philadelphia expressed interest in bringing me on for another year. Though I'd turn thirty-nine in July, I still felt strong and capable of playing good football. But when I thought and prayed about it, I knew I couldn't uproot my family yet again. Timon was six, already in school, and the twins had just turned two. I had bigger priorities than extending my football career. Maybe it was appropriate to end my NFL life that way. The first team I played for was the Buccaneers, at J. L. Long Middle School, and so was the last one.

I wanted my football career to end with the Raiders, though, and fortunately they agreed. At a press conference on July 18, 2005, I signed a ceremonial contract with the team and announced my retirement from football. Chester McGlockton, Marcus Allen, and Lincoln Kennedy were there. So were current Raider Jerry Porter and team officials Amy Trask, Marc Badain, and Mike Taylor. Al Davis didn't make it.

It had been an amazing run. I walked away satisfied that I'd given my all on the football field. I hadn't played for personal records but to be part of something bigger, helping my teammates also become the best they could be while trying to win every time we stepped between the lines. It was difficult to leave the game knowing I'd never tasted a championship, not just in the NFL but at any level. On the other hand, I knew if I felt that way, I still had the right perspective.

18

A FATHER LEADS HIS CHILDREN

It is a wise father that knows his own child.

WILLIAM SHAKESPEARE

When I retired, people like John Elway and Michael Jordan advised me to enjoy it yet to also pursue other interests. I knew that finding a job wasn't going to be a problem. I joined Fox Sports Net that fall as a broadcaster. I also investigated ownership possibilities with NASCAR, although the economic crash prevented us from securing enough funds to get it launched.

One of the best things about my retirement, though, is that it gave me a new opportunity to focus on my family. I love each of my kids in a way that words can't describe. If you're a parent, you know what I mean. They are a part of me. We have a bond that can never be broken.

I'm sure every father who's involved in his children's lives feels that way. I've observed, however, a trend in parenting today that bothers me. Too often, I see dads (moms too) who try to be buddies with their kids. They act as if they and their children are equals. They're so concerned about keeping the kids smiling and satisfied in the moment that they say yes to whatever their kids want, even though they need to be thinking about the long term and sometimes saying no. In our society today, it seems everything is available and permissible in terms of language, alcohol, drugs, and sex. Kids need clear guidance from someone in authority to steer them through that. Fathers shouldn't try to be friends with their kids. A dad should be the leader of his family.

Not long ago, I had a conversation about this with my daughter Timon. She'd just turned fourteen. She's a fantastic kid who almost always makes good decisions, but with boys already in the picture and all the other teenage temptations looming, I knew the road ahead was sure to have bumps. I needed to remind her who had the keys to the car.

"Timon," I said, "for the next six or seven years, we may not like each other very much. I just want you to know that I'm fine with that. You don't have to like what I say. In fact, the less you like it, the better I may be doing as your dad. All I need you to do is listen to me and follow what I say and I'll get you through this."

My daughter looked at me like I'd lost my mind, but that's okay. Sometimes a dad's role is to be the no-fun parent.

I tell my kids, "Life is a rope. You get to grab hold and swing it from the tree as high and far as you can. If you can manage that, I'll stand back and guide you from there. But if the rope starts to choke you, I need to jump in and swing it for you."

I don't see myself as a strict disciplinarian, but I do try to establish boundaries for my children. I want them to understand what they're supposed to do and not do. I have no desire to check their cell phones every day or control their every decision, but if I see behavior that doesn't line up with what I expect, I'm more than willing to step in.

Taylor was always a straight-up kid. I never had to worry about drugs or underage drinking or those kinds of issues. When he was twelve, though, there was a time when he talked disrespectfully to people in authority over him. I'd heard that he sassed his teacher at vacation Bible school. When I asked him about it, his flippant answer was, "Oh, yeah, I did that," as if it was no big deal.

I needed to take action right then or the problem was only going to get worse. So what did I do? I punched Taylor right in the chest—not hard enough to hurt him, but hard enough to get his attention. Believe me, it worked! It helped him realize that he was out of line and I wasn't going to tolerate it. We talked some more and I never had that trouble with him again.

Am I saying that anytime you have a problem with your children that you should punch them? Of course not. A dad's discipline has to fit the crime and the kid. You have to know your children and know what's going to be most effective as a teaching tool—what works for our family might not work for yours. At the time, Taylor was almost as big as me, nearly six feet tall. He already knew what I expected, so more words wouldn't be enough by themselves. He was too old for a time-out or a spanking. To show him I was serious, I felt I needed to make a physical statement—and if that left him wondering what his crazy dad would do the next time he crossed the line, that was fine too.

I don't enjoy disciplining my kids. I do it because I love them and I know it will pay off for them in the long run. The trick is figuring out the right method for each child at the time, because every child is unique.

Timothy and Tamar, who we often call Mar-Mar, are perfect examples of this. Even though they're twins, we have to take completely different approaches to disciplining them. Timothy likes to please. When he makes a mistake, he'll say, "Dad, I know. I shouldn't have done that." He wants nothing to do with a spanking. He'll do anything to avoid that belt.

Tamar is another story. One night when she was just four, she came into the bedroom where Sherice and I were sleeping. Even though she'd been doing fine sleeping in her own room, she'd suddenly decided she wanted to stay in the bed with us. "Tamar," I said, "you have a bed and a beautiful room of your own. You need to sleep there." I picked her up and put her back in her bed.

Tamar had a fit: "I don't want to go in my room! I don't want to go in my room!" Ninety minutes later, she was still screaming. Something had to be done. After what seemed like a hundred warnings, I finally pulled out my belt and popped her a couple of times on her behind—nothing too hard, you understand, just enough to get the point across. (Again, you may find another method of discipline that's more appropriate for your family.)

For most kids, and certainly for Timothy, that would have been enough to take care of the situation. But not for Tamar. She stopped yelling, looked at me calmly, and said, "Are you done? Why don't you get Mommy and have her whip me too, because after you guys are done I'm still coming into your room."

Wow. That belt didn't mean a thing to this child. What was more, she was challenging me. Now it was a battle of wills. I *had* to win this one and show her who had the authority or we'd have problems for the rest of our years together.

Tamar's bedroom had more than one exit, so this time I picked her up and put her in another bedroom, which had just one door. I told her she could scream all she wanted, but she wasn't going to sleep in Mommy and Daddy's bedroom. I sat in the room with her, my back against the door, while she hollered. I eventually fell asleep there. Four hours later—yes, you read that right—she finally calmed down and woke me up. "Daddy, I'm sorry," she said. "I'll go to bed now. I'm sorry."

We had to get up at six o'clock the next morning. When I woke up Tamar in her bed, she smiled and said, "Hi, Daddy, how are you?" as if nothing had happened. It had been a very long night, but I'd learned important lessons on how to discipline and not discipline Tamar, while she'd learned that I wasn't going to back down when she challenged me.

Anyone who says parenting is easy doesn't have a kid of his own.

There are all kinds of philosophies on raising kids. I know many people are against any kind of corporal punishment. All I can say is that when I grew up, everybody in my neighborhood got whipped or spanked when they disobeyed their parents, including me. I never got a whipping I didn't deserve and I hate to think about what I might have done if I thought I never had to face my dad's belt. My father was far from perfect, but other than the night he threatened to kill me, I think the way he handled family discipline was just about right.

A spanking isn't effective for every child, and absolutely you have to be careful about it. If you're angry, you need to calm down before you do anything physical. A spanking should be a rare occurrence, used only when your child defies you or ignores repeated warnings. It should sting only a little, and a couple of swats are all you need. And the older your kids get, the better it is to find another discipline option. These days in the Brown household, that might mean taking away the cell phone and other electronic devices, saying no to friends coming over or trips to the mall, and removing swimming pool privileges for a day or two.

Discipline shouldn't be a dirty word. The Bible says that "He who spares the rod hates his son, but he who loves him is careful to discipline him" (Prov. 13:24). I don't need to be friends with my kids. I need to be their dad.

I've probably given the impression that I'm a stern taskmaster who's always watching for my children to step over the line. That's not me at all. Even though I do have expectations and respond quickly if they're not met, I try to balance that with lots of love and connection.

I travel often, but when I'm home I spend as much time with my kids as I can. That's one area where I'm trying to be different than my dad. My father was always either working or recovering from work, so he didn't have time or energy to be involved in the lives of his children. Whether it's coaching one of their teams, attending their events, driving them to school or practice, or just hanging out at home, I aim to be around my kids. And of course we're together at church whenever I'm in town.

Just as my kids have their own individual responses to different methods of discipline, they're also individuals when it comes to what they enjoy and how they connect. Timon is our touchy-feely girl. Sometimes you can talk and talk to her and never get a conversation started, but if you rub her head or her back, she'll open up. I try to give her extra hugs or do silly things like "accidentally" bump into her. Physical touch is what brings her out of her shell.

Timothy, on the other hand, is all about getting time with Mom and Dad. He'll walk into my office and say, "When are we going to have a Daddy day?" He loves board games and playing any kind of ball. The best way to show Tamar that we love her, meanwhile, seems to be through gifts. Buy her some clothes or a snow cone and she'll light up like a Christmas tree. The point is that each one is unique, so Sherice and I try to parent them accordingly.

My kids all love to travel. We take at least one family trip a year to Lake Tahoe, which is always a great chance for us to enjoy being together. We also consistently include the kids in extended family gatherings—and we have a lot of them. My mom, brother, and sisters all live within two miles of each other, so we get together every Monday night at Mama's house for dinner and catching up. Timon is part of a competitive cheerleading squad now, so she can't make it as often, but over the years the kids have had a lot of time and fun with their grandparents and aunts and uncles and seen the value of a close extended family.

The Brown family's competitive spirit comes out two or three times a year when we all get together at my house for a game night. I'm not talking about cards and board games. We take it to another level, based on the TV show *Minute to Win It*. We divide into two teams and use stuff you can find around the house to see who can prevail in sixty-second contests. It might be flicking cards into a trash can, bouncing Ping-Pong balls across a table, or balancing items on your head. On a typical game night, we might have thirty family members there, men and boys versus women and girls.

Believe me, it's intense. I pull out a bunch of old uniforms so all the guys are wearing number eighty-one. In each category, one contestant from each team faces off on our racquetball court, where everyone else can watch them through the glass. We have a referee too. You better believe there's a lot of cheering and yelling, not to mention a little trash talk. It's all a good time, and the best part is that no matter how young or old, everyone participates.

People say I was a leader on the Raiders. It was a role I grew into, but once I became a team captain and had the opportunity, it was a challenge I took seriously. I tried to be a link between coaches and the younger players who weren't always sure what was what. I talked with other staff in the organization to stay in the loop on what was happening. I served as a players union representative. Most of the time, people seemed to appreciate what I did. If I was going to be a team leader, I wanted to do it to the best of my ability.

None of what I did as a leader with the Raiders, however, is even a fraction as important as what I do as the head of my family. The influence I have on my kids is powerful. For better and worse, it may extend for generations. That's why, as in everything else, I lean heavily on God to show me the way.

Scripture says, "Fathers, do not exasperate your children; instead, bring them up in the training and instruction of the Lord" (Eph. 6:4). That's a verse I take to heart. All the love and discipline I impart to my children will only go so far. More than anything else, I want to lead them to a love for and relationship with God. Just like Mama did with me and my siblings, Sherice and I make sure our kids are in church as often as possible.

Recently, Timon asked me if she could attend a music event for kids in downtown Dallas. I eventually said yes, but not before I secured a promise from her to lock in more at church. "The more church you get, the more it frees me to say yes to these kinds of things," I said. "When you get God in you, it reassures me that you know how to handle situations when you're away from us."

Going to church doesn't guarantee a relationship with God, of course. But the more you expose your kids to what God and His Word are all about, the more likely they are to understand Him and invite Him into their hearts. That's what I'm after—to get God into my kids. I believe that's what any dad should be after. When he does that, he has become a true leader.

19

A MAN OVERCOMES EVIL

If it is an extraordinary blindness to live without investigating what we are, it is a terrible one to live an evil life, while believing in God.

BLAISE PASCAL

I played against a few mean dudes in my time in the NFL—defenders who couldn't wait for a chance to rip someone's head off. You could say those guys were the enemy when I lined up against them. But they were nothing compared to the ultimate enemy we all face in this life. You've probably heard of him. I'm talking about the deceiver . . . the destroyer . . . the prince of darkness . . . the devil. Evil personified.

Many people don't like to talk about demons or the devil. Some would rather not acknowledge that evil even exists. But I've been aware of evil since that day I saw it prayed out of my cousin back at our little Victory Chapel church in Dallas. I know the devil is out there and actively working to take us down. He has all kinds of methods. One of his most effective is to set us against each other.

We're all children of God, but conflict between us is as old as Cain and Abel. That's why what God says about it is so important to me: "If it is possible, as far as it depends on you, live at peace with everyone. Do not take revenge, my friends, but leave room for God's wrath. . . . Do not be overcome by evil, but overcome evil with good" (Rom. 12:18–19, 21).

I've already told you about the night I was almost thirteen when I surprised my dad in the den and he threatened to use his gun on me. I can't help wondering if the devil himself was at work in the rift that developed between us. For sure it was evil because nothing was the same with my dad and me after that night. I was mad and hurt. He was distant and quick to put me down. For years—through my time in high school, college, and the early years of the NFL—he would walk out of the room when I walked in. The great relationship we'd both enjoyed when I was young had vanished.

All through that period, I tried hard to please him and get his attention. I was constantly wondering, *Will this be the game he notices? Will this be the season that gets him back? Will this be the year he apologizes for what happened?* But winning the Heisman didn't do it. Neither did landing in my first Pro Bowl. Neither did getting hurt in my second year with the Raiders.

After the 1991 season, I was chosen for my second Pro Bowl. I felt fully recovered from the knee injury that had sidelined me in 1989. I was almost twenty-six years old and feeling good again about what I could do on the field. The chill I still felt at home, however, made all of that seem hollow. I wanted more than my football skills back. After thirteen years of being pushed away, I wanted my dad back.

What I finally realized that offseason was that my father was too reserved, too stubborn, and too proud to tell me after all those years that he was sorry for what he'd done and what had happened with us. Like many men of his generation, that was just who he was. As much as he might have wanted to say those things, he was incapable of it. I decided that if I was going to have a relationship with him again, I had to go to him.

In the summer of 1992, I had my chance. He was in his garage, which he'd converted into his personal space. He had a TV, a fridge, and a cabinet where he kept food, guns, and whatever else he thought he needed. His favorite spot was in the corner, sitting on top of four or five plastic lawn chairs stacked together and fluffed with pillows. That's where he was when I walked in, took a deep breath, and looked him in the eyes.

"Look, man," I said, "what happened thirteen years ago is over. Let's let bygones be bygones. I need you to be my father. I need you in my life. I forgive you for what happened and if you need to forgive me for whatever I've done, then forgive me. We need to let this go and move on." I put my hand out.

As I've said, my dad was a man of few words, but if he disagreed with you, he definitely let you know about it. When he took my hand and said in his husky voice, "All right, man, all right," I knew he wanted a change too.

From that point on, our relationship was back to normal. Whenever I visited, I joined him in the garage to watch TV or just shoot the breeze. He acted as if we'd never had an issue. Whether it was the devil that had divided us or just plain human foolishness, we'd put an end to it. We were father and son again.

———

Not all conflict is evil, but conflict was definitely part of my dealings with another important man in my life—Al Davis. You could say that my relationship with the Raiders owner was complicated.

I heard soon after I joined the Raiders that Al had not wanted to draft me, that he'd reluctantly gone along with the decision of his staff. When I saw him and Mike Shanahan going at it verbally on the sidelines in my rookie year, I knew our owner wasn't afraid to express his opinions. Al had been head coach and general manager of the Raiders in the sixties, when he coined his motto "Just win, baby," and even served briefly as commissioner of the American Football League before buying into and taking control of the Raiders. He was passionate about football and his team, and expected people to produce. He had his way of doing things and didn't care if others liked it or not.

He could be difficult, that's for sure. After a contract dispute with Marcus Allen, he called Marcus a "cancer on the team." For the next two seasons, Al directed that Marcus's playing time be reduced until he finally released him. He and I had our own tough contract negotiations and conversations over the years. Early in my career, Al wanted me to be a specialist—a kick returner and third-down receiver—while I wanted to play regularly. In 1993, during the last year of my contract at the time, he got on quarterback Vince Evans after a game for throwing the ball to me too much. He made a similar statement to quarterback Jeff George in 1998.

Yet there was a side to Al that people didn't often see. He could be supportive and loyal to his current players and especially to retired Raiders, putting in a good word for them when they needed a job recommendation or giving money to a guy with a medical problem. After I retired, he invested in my Locker 81 company, which raises funds for nonprofit organizations. Obviously, that's something he didn't have to do.

When I played, I talked to Al at least briefly every week and he always listened to what I had to say. We had our disagreements, but they were never personal. It was always related to football. On the rare occasions when I asked for more time with him, he made himself available. When my contract expired after the 1993 season, I thought Al wanted me gone. I signed a four-year offer sheet for $11 million from Denver and figured my years as a Raider were over. But to my surprise, Al matched the offer six days later. We sat down soon after for a six-hour meeting. I went through a list of questions to try to figure out where he was coming from regarding me, my role with the team, and the organization. To his credit, Al answered every question. For that brief time, I felt we understood each other.

I believe Al's philosophy was that the right players on defense were critical to success and players on offense could be replaced. I certainly never felt like I was his guy. I have to admit, though, that the things Al said or orchestrated gave me an edge on the field and in the locker room. I wanted to prove him wrong when he criticized me. It was almost like how I tried to get approval from my dad. I wanted Al to say, "Tim, you're truly a Raider now. You really do care about the organization." Unfortunately, that never happened.

After my difficult separation from the Raiders in 2004, I hardly ever saw or talked to Al again. I wish that had been different. In 2008, at a Raiders game in Oakland, I did try to go up to his suite to say hello to him. I was told Al said, "Come back later." I didn't.

I had a brief conversation with Al at the Raiders facilities in 2009 when I was going in and he was leaving. That was the last time I saw him. He died in 2011 at age eighty-two. No matter what else you want to say about Al Davis, he was one of the great figures in the history of football. He gave his heart and soul to the Raiders and I'm grateful he gave me the opportunity to be part of that.

I had my conflicts with Al, but at least I usually knew where he was coming from. In 1996, I suddenly faced a conflict that I never saw coming. This one sure felt like the devil's handiwork. At an industry trade show, the shoe company I'd founded received commitments from major retailers of close to $20 million in shoe orders. Our company, Pro Moves, was doing great and poised to take another big step forward. I was pleased to be making money, of course, but I was also excited because I thought we were doing something good. By offering high-quality shoes at a lower price than other retailers, we were providing people with a first-rate product that many couldn't afford otherwise.

Apparently, our efforts made someone uncomfortable. Just a few days after the trade show and with no explanation, our manufacturer informed us that they would no longer produce our line of shoes. We were stunned. We scrambled to find another manufacturer, but it was too late. In the shoe business, if you miss a delivery, you're finished. Our business imploded and I lost millions. We even tried to unload our shoes to a network of pawn shops across the nation. That didn't work either.

I soon found out what had happened. Representatives of one of the country's biggest shoe manufacturers and retailers decided they wanted us out of the business. They threatened other major retailers, saying to each that if they didn't stop selling our line they would pull *their* line from that firm's stores. They also intervened with our manufacturer. It was business-style blackmail. They even blocked our plan to sell in the pawn shops.

As you might expect, I was furious. I stayed angry for a long time. If I'd continued to hold on to that anger, it easily could have turned into bitterness and distrust that would have poisoned me and my relationships with my friends and family. But after a lot of prayer, I sensed God telling me that He had *allowed* this to happen. Something I often tell people is that God allows bad things to happen to us for a reason. If it's so bad that it takes us out, we're dead and gone and the lesson is for someone else. But if we're still standing at the end of it, the lesson is for us.

I was reeling but still standing after our shoe business collapsed, so I decided I'd better look for the lesson. I realized that if Pro Moves had kept expanding, I surely would have retired early from football to manage the company. I might have made a lot more money than I did in the NFL, but I wouldn't have had nearly the same visibility and opportunities I have now to speak about God with youth and families. The failure of my shoe company made it possible for me to better serve Him.

By showing me what He'd allowed and why, God prevented me from spiraling into bitterness and steered me onto a more productive path. For me, it was another example of changing what was intended as evil and meant to harm me into something good.

Today, I still run up against conflicts, challenges, and the temptation to repay evil for evil, but I'm learning to give that over to God. Recently, I was driving with Timon and we planned to stop for a bite at a burger joint. We turned left at a light and pulled into the restaurant parking lot. Apparently, the young woman driving a car toward me in the opposite direction felt I'd cut her off. She gave me an obscene gesture as she pulled in behind me.

I was surprised, but I planned to let it go. Then, while inside the restaurant and standing in line to order, I noticed the young woman's boyfriend was right behind me. In a polite voice, I turned to him and said, "Hey brother, I apologize for going in front of you there, but you really should keep your girlfriend from flipping folks off. You just never know when it's going to be the wrong person. People get killed over that kind of thing."

I was surprised a second time when the boyfriend, who was a little bigger than me, went off. "What you gonna do?" he shouted at me. "What you gonna do, bro?" Heads turned in the restaurant.

I had no desire to mess with some crazy dude, especially with my daughter there. I turned and took a few steps away.

"Oh, you *better* walk away," he said loudly.

I whipped back around. Now I was being mocked. That NFL competitive fire was rising up in me faster than steam in a teapot. Suddenly, all I could see was me punching this guy in the face and maybe breaking his nose.

That's when I stopped for an extra split second to get another opinion. It took every ounce of God I had in me, but I let Him take control. He made it clear what I needed to do. Instead of jumping into the macho man thing and teaching this guy a lesson, I took a deep breath and turned around again. Timon and I sat down at a table to eat. The confrontation was over.

I'm not trying to say how godly I am here. I don't always win that spiritual battle. But it is another example of how we can take a stand against and overcome evil if we stop trying to handle everything ourselves and instead allow God's Spirit to run the show.

There's a type of evil that's more subtle than a threatening boyfriend. It's the kind that fools people into thinking they can follow God while also keeping one foot in the craziness of this world. I see it all the time. Hey, I know it's tough to stand up and stand out for your faith. But there's no middle ground. Either you're on the team or you're not. Either you proudly wear the jersey or you're embarrassed and you take it off. So why not be who you really are, wherever you are? God says, "But if serving the LORD seems undesirable to you, then choose for yourselves this day whom you will serve" (Josh. 24:15).

If you want to blend in with everyone else and live like the world, go for it. But don't call yourself a Christian. As my pastor has said many times, there's no place in the Bible where people are called to follow Jesus but *aren't* called to change their ways. The change may not be immediate, but as soon as you invite Jesus into your life, He starts going to work on you. You learn to give up the "old man" and take on the new—at least, that's how it's supposed to work.

This is huge for the Christian believer because it has to do with eternal salvation—whether we go to heaven or not. People debate with me about it, saying that even after we ask for Christ's forgiveness and commit ourselves to Him, we still all sin every day and that God's grace covers it. That, in other words, our ticket is still punched. Well, it's true that we still make mistakes, me definitely included, and that God's grace makes up for it. But it's one thing to try to follow Jesus and screw up, and another to deliberately turn your back on Him. The Bible puts it plainly: "If we deliberately keep on sinning after we have received the knowledge of the truth, no sacrifice for sins is left, but only a fearful expectation of judgment and of raging fire that will consume the enemies of God" (Heb. 10:26–27).

God loved me just as much before I committed my life to Him as He does now. But just because He loves me doesn't mean I have a seat in His eternal family if I walk away from Him. He's a loving God but also a just God. Whatever we say or do, He knows what's in our hearts.

I told you that as a boy, I dreamed of growing up to be a preacher. That didn't happen, but I must have at least a little preacher in me, because I get pretty upset when I think about these things. I hate to see the devil delude people, and I hate to see those I know and care about miss out on the glory of heaven.

I know I'm getting older, because I think about these matters more—what happens when we die and what kind of legacy we'll leave behind. That's what I want to talk about in our last chapter.

20

YOUR LEGACY
MATTERS

A life is not important except in the impact it has on other lives.

JACKIE ROBINSON

In 2001, my dad had surgery to put stents in his coronary arteries. His doctor told him that if he gave up smoking, there was no doubt he'd live until he was ninety. I bought him patches and electronic cigarettes to help him quit, and he did give it up—for about a month. For my dad, it was more about having something in his hand than the actual smoking. Even so, he just couldn't stop.

He was still smoking late in 2008 when his breathing got so bad and his blood so poisoned with carbon monoxide that he had to go to the hospital. He was diagnosed with chronic obstructive pulmonary disease. There was no cure. His health was never good after that. In April 2011, I told him I wanted him to come to my house for Mother's Day. He said, "Son, I'm not going to be here for Mother's Day."

Two days before Mother's Day, on May 6, 2011, my father fell down at home and suffered a contusion to the head. He died later that day. Eugene Brown was seventy-five years old. His funeral procession looked like one for a head of state—it included eight presidential-sized limousines, as well as other limos. It was one of the biggest processions the local funeral home had ever handled. That was my dad. He drew people from all walks of life. At my mom's house after the funeral, it was amazing to see so many grown men, both young and old, break down crying and say how much my dad helped them and how much they'd miss him.

We included a plaque in my dad's casket that read, simply, "Patriarch." That was his role in our large, close family and was how we all planned to remember him. In his closet, we'd found a neatly folded T-shirt. It had my picture on it and the words "1987 Heisman Trophy Winner." He'd saved it for all those years. I had them put it on him to wear under his burial clothes.

It hurt then to lose my dad and still does. The pain was fresher then but is deeper now. I miss him and can't believe he's gone. But I'm so glad that we repaired our relationship and got to enjoy each other the last nineteen years of his life.

I'm also so grateful for the Lord's intervention and the faithful efforts of a ninety-year-old woman in our church. About a year and a half before my dad's death, a woman we called "Mother Page" told my mom that the Lord had laid it on her heart to talk to my father. When Mama mentioned this to me and my siblings, we said, "Oh, no, Mama, don't subject Mother Page to that."

Mama did try to thank Mother Page for her interest while gently discouraging her. Mother Page wasn't going to be put off, however. "You must have misunderstood what I said," she told Mama. "The *Lord* said for me to talk to your husband." This time, Mama went home and told my dad about it. "Well," he said, "give her my number."

To the rest of the family's amazement, Mother Page started praying over the phone with my father two times a day. In the last couple months of his life, my mom was surprised several times to walk into a room and see my father on his knees, praying. The night before he died, he told my mom he was "all right with God." If that's not a blessing, I don't know what is.

On a morning six months after my dad passed, I was driving my kids to school when my phone rang. "Where are you?" Sherice asked.

"What do you mean, where am I?" I said. "I'm dropping off the kids."

"Are you coming right back?"

"Sure," I said. "I've still got my pajamas on. Where do you think I'm going?"

When I pulled up to my house, Sherice met me at the door. *Oh, Lord*, I thought. My first concern was Mama, but family would have called me fifteen times by now if something had happened to her.

Sherice took me upstairs and broke the news: "Chester passed away." He'd suffered a massive heart attack.

I couldn't believe it. I'd just talked to Chester two days before. He was planning to visit us the next week. He was only forty-two years old, with a wife and two daughters at home. How could this have happened?

I was really broken. I wanted to tear up the house. My buddy was suddenly gone and I didn't know how to handle it. It just didn't seem real.

My time with Chester was the same as the second good phase of my relationship with my dad: nineteen years. It's amazing that anyone can love a big, ornery defensive tackle, but I did. I can't get those years and great memories back, but I can be thankful for them and look forward to the day we meet again on the other side of this life.

After going through such painful losses, I was very aware that no one can guarantee how long we and the people we care about will be on this earth. But it was reinforced even more in May 2012 when I got a call telling me that Junior Seau had taken his own life. Again, I was shocked. I'd seen Junior at my golf tournament only two days earlier and watched him laugh and joke with his golf partners.

It was a contrast, actually, from when I'd seen Junior in March while playing in his golf tournament. I noticed then that he drank throughout the day. At the reception at the end of that tournament, he kept slurring his words. It was bad enough that I couldn't watch; I walked out of the room. I was concerned. Later, I hatched a plan with Marcus Allen to sit down with Junior at my tournament, talk to him about his drinking, and see if we could help. But then Marcus had a conflict and couldn't make my tournament. We decided to wait until Marcus's tournament that was only three weeks later.

Now it was too late. My emotions were jumbled. I was sad to have lost another friend, angry that Junior had done this to his family and friends, and upset that I'd missed my chance to speak to him. Would it have made any difference? I don't know. We've all since learned that Junior's problems were more complex than I'd realized, that he was in debt and apparently suffered from a form of brain damage, a far too common condition among professional football players. I believe it's often the combination of personal struggles and brain issues that are pushing football players to take their own lives. Obviously, we need more study on this. But when I got the news about Junior, I wasn't thinking about any of that. I just couldn't believe that another great NFL player and friend was gone.

Life is so brief, and what we do while we're alive is often quickly forgotten. In 2003, Ukranian swimmer Andriy Serdinov achieved his lifelong goal by setting the world record in the 100-meter butterfly. Naturally, he was overjoyed—he celebrated by throwing his hands into the air. Five minutes later, he was in the middle of his first interview as the record holder when an eighteen-year-old American named Michael Phelps swam even faster, setting a new world mark for the event. Serdinov never held a world record again.

That's how life is. We sacrifice and strive to reach the pinnacle of our profession, and if we're fortunate, it garners us rewards such as respect, fame, and financial prosperity. Yet it's all temporary. None of it truly lasts.

I'm proud of my football achievements in college and in the NFL. It's an honor to be listed among the great players who have won the Heisman Trophy. It's rewarding to know that when I retired from the NFL, I was second in total receiving yards, third in career catches, tied for third in touchdown catches, and fifth in all-purpose yards. Of course I'm proud of setting NFL records such as consecutive games started by a wide receiver (176), consecutive games with more than one reception (143), and consecutive seasons with at least seventy-five receptions (10).

But when I look back on my life at the end of my days, will any of that truly matter?

At this writing, I've been eligible four times for induction into the NFL Hall of Fame. I've been a finalist a couple of times, but so far the selection committee hasn't recorded the votes to make it happen. Would I like to be in the Hall of Fame? Absolutely. I wouldn't be honest if I said anything else. The Hall would be the final stamp on my career, a chance to see my name among the greatest in the history of the game. Who wouldn't cherish an achievement like that?

Yet I understand that the purpose of my life isn't about getting into the NFL Hall of Fame. The reason I'm on this earth is to serve God; to be the best husband, father, son, brother, and friend I can be; and to lead people to Christ. These are the things that matter. These are the things that last.

When I was a boy, I was impressed by the incredible story of

Jackie Robinson. When Branch Rickey, general manager of the Brooklyn Dodgers, was looking for a man to break baseball's color barrier, he settled on Robinson. "Mr. Rickey," Jackie said at their famous meeting in 1945, "do you want a ballplayer who is afraid to fight back?" No, Rickey responded, "I want a ballplayer with guts enough *not* to fight back."[1] Jackie was an aggressive guy, but when he started playing with the Dodgers in 1947, he took all the insults and hate without retaliating. He forced people to respect him as a great player and as a man.

I was particularly blown away when I read about the life and achievements of Martin Luther King Jr. The risks he took and the faith and fortitude he showed in thrusting civil rights into the national consciousness not only were inspiring but changed history. Through his speeches, his peace marches, and so much more, he left a legacy that still has a powerful impact on us today.

These men put their very lives on the line to make a difference. They understood what will last. When talking about how he wanted to be remembered, Pastor King said, "I'd like somebody to mention that day that Martin Luther King Jr. tried to give his life serving others. . . . If you want to say that I was a drum major, say that I was a drum major for justice. Say that I was a drum major for peace. I was a drum major for righteousness. And all of the other shallow things will not matter."[2]

The leader of my home church in Dallas, Pastor Whitley, is another man who is leaving an important legacy. He's encouraging people to live a godly life, never backing away from the truth of the Bible. I wonder how many men, women, and children have done the right thing over the years because of his preaching and example.

God doesn't call every man to change nations or lead a congregation, but we all influence the lives we come across for better or worse. It's critical that we understand what's important. I'm certainly not in the same category as the men I've just mentioned, but I am trying to live in a way that serves others and pleases God.

For the past twenty years, I've been involved with the nonprofit Athletes and Entertainers for Kids (AEFK). The annual Celebrity Classic golf tournament I cohost with Kathy Ireland raises funds for 9-1-1 for Kids, an AEFK national outreach program that teaches kids how to properly call 911 in an emergency and also educates youth and their families on how to respond to an emergency or disaster.

I've also established Locker 81 Fundraising Solutions, a company that sponsors a program called Smart Giving Cards. When people use a Smart Giving debit card for everyday purchases, it raises money for nonprofits such as the National Council of Youth Sports. We've formed the Tim Brown Foundation, which in the past has sponsored a program for latchkey kids in the Dallas area. We hope to get that back up and running soon.

Recently, we also got involved with Five Star Life, a nonprofit organization based in Indiana that builds self-esteem and character in middle school kids. We plan to help establish a Five Star program in Texas.

That's more than enough to fill my plate, but we've also launched a business venture called Smart Living. It promotes health and wellness through enzyme-based products that are 100 percent natural. And I keep in touch with the sports world through my football radio shows on SiriusXM.

As I've said, I love kids, so the chance to improve their lives through many of the programs I'm involved in is especially rewarding for me. Of course, the kids closest to my heart are the ones I have the privilege to call my own: Taylor, Timon, Tamar, and Timothy. I include another young woman in that list too. Ratisha is Sherice's twenty-two-year-old cousin. Her parents were both killed, so we've been raising her in our home since she was eleven. Now she's working and taking some classes in the Dallas area, which is great.

When I look to the future, what do I want for my kids? Obviously I want them to grow as people of character, to prosper, to be great citizens, to give back as much as they can to this world. But more than any of that, I want them to love and serve God. That's living a life that matters. As Pastor Whitley has said, even if God's promise of heaven weren't true, what a great life we live when we serve Him. When I get to the end of my days, if I can see each member of my family honoring God and doing His will, then I'll know I have a legacy to be proud of.

You might wonder how I want to be remembered. Yes, as a player who gave his all on the football field. Certainly as someone who loved and led his family. Even more than that, though, I'd like to be remembered as a guy who was faithful to God and his beliefs, who was consistent in the way he lived and served others. These are the things that make a man.

When I reach the end of my life, I hope to be able to say the same words that the apostle Paul once wrote to my namesake, Timothy:

> I have fought the good fight, I have finished the race, I have kept the faith. Now there is in store for me the crown of righteousness, which the Lord, the righteous Judge, will award to me on that day—and not only to me, but also to all who have longed for his appearing. (2 Tim. 4:7–8)

NFL CAREER STATS

- At time of retirement 14,934 receiving yards were second-highest total in NFL history; 1,094 receptions were 3rd; and 100 touchdown catches were tied for 3rd
- Total of 19,682 combined net yards, 5th all-time at time of retirement
- NFL all-time ranks: 14,934 receiving yards (6th), 100 receiving touchdowns (Tie – 7th), 1,094 receiving (5th)
- Scored 105 total touchdowns (100 receiving, 1 rushing, 3 punt returns, 1 kickoff return)
- Voted to Pro Bowl nine times, 1989 and 1992 as kick returner, 1994-98, 2000 and 2002 as a receiver
- As rookie led NFL in kickoff returns, return yards, and yards per return average
- Led NFL in receptions, 1997

- Set Raiders franchise records for receptions, receiving yards, and punt return yards
- All-Pro choice as a kick returner, 1998
- All-Pro wide receiver, 1997
- Was named All-AFC as a kick returner, 1988, punt returner, 1991, and wide receiver, 1993, 1994, 1995, 1997

ACKNOWLEDGMENTS

I can't begin to thank all of the people who have influenced me for the better on this amazing journey. My family, however, deserves special mention for their support, encouragement, and love.

To my wife, Sherice. Thank you for being who you are and for understanding who I am. I can't wait to see what God has in store for us in the years ahead. I love you.

To my son Taylor. I admire the young man you've become and look forward to seeing you grow even more. I'm also looking forward to those grandkids—after you get married, of course!

To my daughter Timon. You've entered that pivotal time of facing life-altering decisions. I know you'll make good ones—but when you're in doubt, please let this book be a guide. It's as much for you as it is for your brothers.

To my daughter Tamar. You have so much potential. Daddy just wants you to grow up to be the wonderful young lady you're meant to be and to keep God close to your heart.

To my son Timothy. Little man, you're the man of our house when I leave. I hope this book helps you become the man of your own house one day.

To Tish, who I'm glad to have as part of our family. Even though some things in life don't make sense, always remember that God is taking care of you and has a tremendous plan for your life.

To my mother, Josephine Brown. Mama, thank you for being such an inspiration in my life. You mean so much to me. I would not be where I am today without you.

To my sisters and brother: Joyce, Ann, Gwen, Kathy, and Wayne. Thank you for being true family instead of fans. You'll never know how much that has meant to me.

To my pastor, Lafayette Whitley. You've always talked to me and taught me from the same point of view. Thank you for being my pastor instead of my pal. You are my spiritual father on earth.

To all my extended family, friends, teammates, coaches and staff, and fans in Raider Nation and elsewhere. You're a part of my life that will always be appreciated and never forgotten.

This book also would not have been possible without the efforts of a few special people.

To Jim Lund, my collaborator. It's been an incredible experience, man. Thank you for your talent in bringing my story to life.

To Joel Kneedler, my agent and Raiders fan extraordinaire, and Debbie Wickwire, my editor and fellow Texan. Thank you for seeing the vision and making that vision a reality.

To John Heisler and Michael Bertsch at Notre Dame, Will Kiss at the Raiders, Brian Curtis, and everyone on the team at Thomas Nelson for their valuable contributions.

Finally, I thank God for giving me the opportunity to serve Him and join His eternal family. This is all for You.

NOTES

CHAPTER 2

1. "Parent's Love Affects Child's Health," Reuters, 10 March 1997, as quoted in James Dobson, *Bringing Up Boys* (Wheaton, IL: Tyndale, 2001), 85.

CHAPTER 12

1. Austin Murphy, "Sweet Moves," *Sports Illustrated*, 6 July 1988, http://sportsillustrated.cnn.com/vault/article/magazine/MAG1013274/index.htm.
2. Gary Chapman, *The Five Love Languages* (Chicago: Northfield, 1992), 15.

CHAPTER 15

1. Anne M. Peterson, "Rice Reborn," Florence, Alabama, *Times Daily*, 26 July 2001, 4D.

CHAPTER 16

1. Bruce Barton, as quoted in John Lloyd and John Mitchinson, *If Ignorance Is Bliss, Why Aren't There More Happy People?* (New York: Harmony, 2008), 313.

CHAPTER 20

1. David Oshinsky, "The Man Who Hired Jackie Robinson," *New York Times Sunday Book Review*, 25 March 2011, BR16.
2. "Events of 1968: Martin Luther King Assassination," upi.com, 1968, http://www.upi.com/Archives/Audio/Events-of-1968/Martin-Luther-King-Assassination/.

ABOUT THE AUTHORS

Tim Brown is one of the greatest wide receivers to ever play in the National Football League. Notre Dame's Heisman Trophy winner in 1987, Tim played sixteen seasons for the Los Angeles and Oakland Raiders, earning nine Pro Bowl selections and setting numerous team and league records. He has served as a television analyst for Fox Sports NBC, ESPN, and Sirius XM Satellite radio, and devotes his time and efforts to numerous charitable causes.

James Lund is an award-winning collaborator and editor and the coauthor of *A Dangerous Faith* and *Danger Calling*. He works with best-selling authors, ministry leaders, and public figures such as Max Lucado, George Foreman, Kathy Ireland, Jim Daly, and Randy Alcorn. Three of his projects earned the Evangelical Christian Publishers Association Gold Medallion Award. Visit his website at www.jameslundbooks.com.